THE
BEGINNING
AND END
OF AN
IMMIGRANT
FAMILY

ANATOLY BEZKOROVAINY

INK START MEDIA
265 Eastchester Dr Ste 133 #102
High Point NC 27262

THE
BEGINNING
AND END
OF AN
IMMIGRANT
FAMILY

ANATOLY BEZKOROVAINY

Mr. Anatoly Bezkorovainy
25449 S. Truro Dr.
Sun Lakes, AZ 85248-6602

THE CONCLUDING STORY

The current booklet is most likely my final piece of written works at the age of 89 years. It was extremely difficult to write it, which I started around the years of 2018-2019 when my wife was still alive (but seriously sick with Parkinson's genetic disease). By the year of 2019 I had most of the story written, but the final part of it I had to continue in the years after she died in 2020. And that is the year when I wrote the book's first original pages, in the 2023rd year, and discarded the ones I had written in the year of 2018-2019 when my wife was still alive. Immediately after her burial I wrote a couple of booklets about her life; published in 2021 was "Marilyn the Mother, Wife, and Teacher," (Author Tranquility Press, Marietta, Georgia) and in 2,022, it was "The Last Call," also published by Authors' Tranquility Press. Both were 153 pages long, and both were written about the life of Marilyn Bezkorovainy, birth name Marilyn Grib. Both books tell the story of Marilyn Grib Bezkorovainy's life, born in 1938, married Anatoly Bezkorovainy's life, born in 1964, and dying in 2020. In her early marriage years, she had two sons (born in 1965 and 1969), who are now superb teachers and writers. Marilyn is buried in Phoenix's main cemetery with the headstone showing both the birth and death years (1938-2020 fig. 01). Anatoly Bezkorovainy is shown to be born in 1935 and his death date being expected only by what the Lord knows. He only prays that the Lord will take him after this current book is published, but after that, the author might decide to write another book and that project will have to be agreed with the Lord.

I tried to write this book four years ago (?), but it somehow did not occur until the year of 2013. At the end of that year, I decided to write my wife's last story and include the initial startup I wrote in 2010. I hope that the book will be published this time (year 2023-2024), and I will happily leave this world whenever the Chairman will decide.

PREFACE FROM 2020

(UNPUBLISHED)

When I turned 80 some time ago, I noticed that my memory was gradually losing its former events much more rapidly than in the past, and many past events were gradually disappearing from my mind, which losses I did not experience with any great joy. And such losses did not easily come back, which I missed miserably. I looked to remember my past and I was beginning to lose it. So what could I do? Many people had started diaries sometime in their youth, others in their Middle Ages... But when they die, their diaries get soon lost since their descendants may not be particularly interested in their ancestors' histories. Others, however, may write novels or stories about tales in their diaries, and yet others may even publish them. But these latter types are very uncommon. So I decided to join these uncommon types and write a story about my wife and me before I die or forget all about our lives. Having a written or even printed record of one's love affair and marriage will not be lost easily and most likely will remain in one's brain until the end of one's life.

I was now and then recalling a life of a colleague of mine of fond memory, whose biography could have been a good story, but because of a love affair it turned out less successful than it could have been. I will briefly relate this story, because a very few times did I have similar feelings in my lifetime, though I did not follow them, and they soon disappeared thereafter, thanks be to God. Here goes: Dr. X was an Australian who had received his doctorate in biochemistry, and after a postdoctoral job, was hired by my Biochemistry Department chairman as Assistant Professor, presumably to help me to handle our 120 medical student Biochemistry course, of which I was the director. I don't know why my boss hired him; he didn't ask me anything about that matter. I had never complained about my work being too hard, nor could I be fired since my title was already Associate Professor and I had tenure, even if my boss wanted to. But to get some help I did not mind, and my boss asked me to help the new Assistant Professor to start his career, including doing research. So I invited him to our research group, and we published a nice group of research papers on transferrin and other topics of my interest. He was a decent researcher, and eventually he was able to get his own grants and run his own research projects. However, I retained my job as a course director for the medical school biochemistry course, which our new Assistant Professor apparently wanted to be a member of. Eventually, I got notice that my colleague was appointed Assistant Dean of the medical school. That job lasted for a year; he got another "promotion" at the Dean's office, and stopped teaching biochemistry. I was promoted to full professor with basically the same jobs, with him giving a couple lectures a year only.

Eventually, my colleague got a national job, I believe, with an organization that makes national medical exams. Then I lost knowledge of his career, but eventually I saw signs on the Illinois highways with Dr. X picture advertising his real estate sales office. He became a real estate sales/buying agent. His private life was also coming along; he came to America with a wife and two little kids, but while working at our medical school, he got into an affair with a graduate student from another department, divorced his wife (I had met her; she was a very nice lady), and married the former graduate student (now a professional person). But the next time I heard about him was that he got sick and died at the age of 60. "Sic transit Gloria mundi…", my father used to say all the time. I was sorry to hear that, after all, he was my colleague… I often thought about him; if he stayed in my department, he would have taken my job as the biochemistry course director when I would have retired (which I did in 2000 A.D. at the age of 65). And then, when my chairman retired in another 2 years, he may have taken over his chairmanship. He was fairly smart and a native English speaker (not like I with a Russian accent): he has all the appropriate properties, but he wanted to reach the top of something sooner than he could have. And he may have avoided getting the cancer disease that killed him.

And so, I am already 86 years old; my former boss and chairman of the Biochemistry Department died 10 years ago, and here I am writing stories about my life's experiences, having buried my beautiful wife in September of the year 2020 A.D., God bless her soul! So why have I chosen to write my Australian colleague's history in the Preface of my book? Perhaps as an excuse to have done less than I could have done in all my life? Perhaps to illustrate what is the maximum success an immigrant with a Slavic English accent can accomplish in America? My readers have perhaps seen all the TV and radio announcers with British/German accents. But how many have seen speakers with a Slavic accent? I haven't seen one in my 70-year life in America. So perhaps I should shut up and be happy with what I have achieved (especially when I think of my department's chairman with the same education as mine, but with a heavy German accent; the poor fellow died of cancer in his trachea). And I, with the grace of God, have lived already 86 years, and yet without any mortal disease threatening. I should not complain about anything; only I still wish that my wife was still alive. She died at the age of 82 of Parkinson's wife's sons will not become victims of their great grandmother's Belorus! I just hope that my and my wife's sons will not become victims of their grandmother's Belorus disease, but will follow my grandmother who died when she was 100+ years old and native of Russia's territory on the Caucasian Mountains.

CHAPTER 1

A BIOGRAPHICAL SKETCH

My father's, lgnatii Bezkorovainy, family had its origins in Ukraine, which, until the Bolshevik revolution in 1917, was a component of Imperial Russia. One of my ancestors had, in fact, been the governor of the Ukrainian province (gubernia/government) of Kherson, and was thus of the Russian nobility class. One of his descendant families, for whatever reason, moved to St. Petersburg, the capital of the Russian Empire, to serve in the Tsar's civil or military services, and in 1873, we find my grandfather (Anatoly Bezkorovainy) graduating from Russia's Imperial Corps of Pages, a military school.

While a student at the Academy, he served as an attendant at the Tsar's court for whatever reason, he did not join the Russian military as a junior officer after graduation, and instead entered Russia's civil service, where he dealt with Russia's railroad transportation systems. He died in his early 50's in 1904 leaving his wife and 5 kids in a somewhat destitute situation. My father was the youngest kid, five years old. My grandmother left St. Petersburg, Russia's capital at that time, to live in the city of Perm, where her family lived and her father was a priest at one of its Orthodox churches. In Perm, she opened a clothing sewing shop, where she was making dresses and suits for the town's inhabitants, thus earning a living for her kids and herself. In Perm, my father graduated from the middle school (gimnazia) around 1917, and entered the local university to study medicine. Why medicine? Because his oldest sister was already a physician and had a great influence on him; and that, because she saved her brother's life when, as a teen ager, he caught typhoid fever because he had drunk a river's water on a hike, and the water was contaminated with the typhoid bacillus. His sister kept him at home and cared for him until he became well. So he studied medicine for a year, and then had to leave Russia because being a male of noble birth was a dangerous property in the Bolshevik environment. Some 2-3 million Russians left their homeland at that time, and my father chose to live in Latvia, just across the border from the Soviet Union. Latvia, along with Estonia and Lithuania, were originally provinces in Imperial Russia, but declared independence in 1918 after Tsarist Russia's collapse. Some 20% of Latvia's inhabitants were Russians, and almost everyone knew how to speak Russian. My father must have felt comfortable there rather than being in France or America, where many Russians had gone after the Bolshevik revolution, and had to learn these foreign languages to survive.

My mother Olga was born in Caucasus, where her father, Alexander Solovey-Pavlichenko, was a salesman of the Singer sewing machine company. He was born in Vieksniai, a Lithuanian province of Imperial Russia. While in the Caucasus, he married my grandmother Anna, whose genetics were, at least in part, those of one of the Caucasian native tribes. During World War I, Alexander was drafted into the Russian army and served on the Turkish front (the Turks were allies of Germany). After the Bolshevik revolution in Russia, he served in the anti-Bolshevik "White" army, which lost the Russian civil war, and with his family, he left Russia for the independent Lithuania to take over his family farm in the Ferma village, near the town of Vieksniai. He stayed there until he passed away in the 1960's. His wife Ann, my grandmother, lived another 25 years to pass on at an age of over 100 years. My mom Olga left Lithuania when she was 16 to 18 years old for Riga, Latvia, where she became an apprentice to learn the beauty culture profession, and she eventually became a licensed beautician. While in Riga, she was supported by the Damberg family, whose husband, Ernest Damberg, was a Latvian businessman married to my grandfather's sister, Elisabeth, Mr. Damberg was of German genetics, whose ancestors were members of the German Knights of the Sword organization, which, on permission of the Pope of Rome, had conquered Latvian and Estonian lands in the 12th century A. D. for the purpose of converting their inhabitants from their pagan religion to Roman Catholicism. The Knights were successful, and established the city of Riga in 1201 A. D. (my birthplace in 1935). For them, the small pieces of land that were populated by Latvians and Estonians were not enough, and they decided to add the lands of Russia to their conquests, all, of course, to the glory of the Roman Pope. They attacked the Russians, who were already Christians since 860's A. D., though not of Roman Catholicism, but of Byzantine Orthodoxy. The Germans failed, and retired back to their Latvian and Estonian lands, and until about 1918, when Latvia and Estonia became independent, the German elite owned most of the land and were basically masters of the Latvian and Estonian native populations who worked for them as their farm hands. Mr. Damberg, a descendant of the Knights of the Sword, did not own any land; he was a modern businessman, who owned a paper factory in Riga, plus several other business entities, and his religion was Orthodox, perhaps on advice of his wife Elisabeth, sister of my grandfather. And lastly, Mr. Damberg was responsible for getting my grandfather out of Russia after the White anticommunist movement collapsed there. Mr. Damberg in 1920 was the Latvian commercial attache in the Moscow Latvian embassy, and he made it possible for my grandfather and his family to leave Soviet Russia to his farm in Lithuania. He and his wife were wonderful human beings, and my parents were in contact with them until they passed away towards the end of the 20th century in Germany where they had remained (while in 1951 we went to America).

In Riga, my mother Olga met my father and the two were married in 1930 in the Alexander Nevsky Orthodox Church. My father was 30 (or 31?) years old and my mom was 20. I was born in 1935, and my brother George in 1938. In 1940, in accordance with the Soviet-German treaty, all 3 Baltic countries (Latvia, Estonia, and Lithuania) were occupied by the Soviets. They began to arrest and execute people as determined by their secret police, the NKVD; my father was a candidate for a knock on the door by them at midnight. He knew that he was on their list because he did not receive a Soviet passport when all Latvian passports were exchanged for Soviet ones as Latvia was officially incorporated into the USSR, except, that is, of folks whom the Soviets considered to be their "enemies." And my father was considered as such because he belonged to a hereditary nobility family of Imperial Russia. So, my father never slept at home, because the Soviets made their political arrests always at night. They caught him. He would have been sent to the Gulag for 10 years, a sentenced prisoner rarely survived. In 1941, World War II started, the Germans occupied Latvia, and my father could again sleep at home.

I have often thought about what were the happiest days of my parents' lives. It seems to me that there weren't too many of them, and I came to the conclusion that these were from 1938 through 1940, and especially, from 1941 through 1944 in Riga, Latvia. During that second stretch, my mother was a master artisan in the female beauty culture industry, earning good money and enjoying her job with multiple friendships with her clients. My dad was working two jobs not because he had to, but because he wanted to: during the day he was an archivist at the state archives institution, and in the evening, he was the financial manager of Riga's Russian drama theater's organization. The latter was a very successful business; he often took us kids to watch the plays, though because of our young ages, we did not understand much of what was going on. We lived on the fifth floor of a large apartment building in a large apartment that had a kitchen with a room next to it for a maid, both my brother and I had our own bedroom as did my parents, and there was a large living-dining room, plus a room which my dad called a "cabinet," where he stored his plentiful private belongings. Since both of my parents worked, we had a maid who cooked and looked after us kids. In 2007, my wife and I were in Riga, Latvia and went to look at my former living quarters. Everything was still there, except an elevator had been added to easier reach the upper floor apartments. Also, the building had been converted into a condo; the costs of the apartments were close to 1 million dollars. Maybe we shouldn't have left Riga in 1944! Before 1941, we lived in a smaller apartment that did not have all the modern equipment that our 1941-1944 apartment had.

In February of 1942 I turned 7, and in September of that year I started going to the first grade (no kindergartens in Latvia) of a Russian-language school. I already knew how to read in the Russian language, and the math was, as I recall, an easy thing to take care of. I had much fun in school; my favorite subject was Religion, which was taught by an Orthodox priest. Most of the students were Orthodox, as I recall, but some were Lutherans (most Latvians were of Lutheran faith, like their Baltic German elite were), and they had a pastor teaching them in a separate class room. On Orthodox feast days, our school's Orthodox students were shipped to Latvia's Orthodox cathedral, which was not far from our school, and everyone attended the services and took communion. I attended this school for two years, and I still remember what I learned, like reading and writing in the Russian language. My third year of school (in fall, 1944) started when we were already in Germany. My little brother did not start school in Riga; his first schooling experience took place in Chemnitz, Germany.

As World War II was proceeding, we had certain issues to worry about, e. g., my father was not too happy to be drafted into the German army, where younger men were taken; the draft had not yet reached men with ages of 40+

years in late 1944, but my father's age of 45 was close enough. Luckily, he was never drafted into the German army. Then there were siren alerts when Soviet planes appeared near or over Riga; usually, they were harmless, but then one never knew... They were never as effective as the British and U.S. airplanes, whose "efficient" bombings we experienced later in Germany. But the worst worry we had was about what would happen if the Germans would lose the war and the Soviets would again take over Latvia; and the future looked bleak indeed. Well, the latter was about to happen toward the end of 1944 and in September, 1944 we decided to leave our home for Germany. After that, life was never as good for my parents as it was in 1938-1940 and 1941-1944 in Riga, Latvia, even though in their old age, they had sufficient means to live in America in reasonable comfort. My dad died in 1975, and my mom passed away at the age of 79 in 1988. They could have lived another 10 years each if they didn't smoke.

And so, in September, 1944 we ascended onto a German military transport ship in the Riga harbor and sailed via the Baltic Sea to Danzig (today's Gdansk, a Polish city). The ship was packed with Latvian refugees, who, like us, were unwilling to live in the Soviet/Communist "paradise," and German soldiers being taken back to their country after being wounded on the Russian front. Soviet airplanes tried to attack the ship, but the ship's anti-aircraft guns and the Russian lack of knowledge on how to sink naval vessels helped us to reach our destination safely. We got off the ship in Danzig and travelled by train to Chemnitz in the Sachsen province of Germany (why Chemnitz, I don't know; we knew no one there). In Chemnitz, we were given a room in a large German apartment building, which was part of an apartment originally occupied by a family, whose male member was a Jew (he had to wear a Star of David sign on his clothing; he was married to a German lady and thus escaped being locked up in a concentration camp like other Jews were). As far as we know, he had survived the holocaust. Our father was given a job as an elevator operator in a German factory, which was supposed to be making sewing machines, but God only knows what they were really making. My mom was allowed to stay home to take care of us kids. Not too long after we settled in our new Chemnitz abode, a surprise took place in our lives: my brother and I were walking with our mother on the street near our house when all of a sudden, we met Uncle Ernest Dam berg walking in the opposite direction. He was looking for our living quarters (there were no phones in private homes at that time). His family had been living in Posen (Polish city Poznan today) since 1940, where his family had moved when the Soviets occupied Latvia in 1940. According to the Ribbentrop-Molotov Treaty between Germany and the USSR, all Baltic States' Germans were allowed to move out of there to Germany and they did. They were settled in the city of Posen which was occupied by the Germans at that time. And now, the Soviet armies had besieged Posen and the former Baltic Germans had to flee again. The Dambergs knew where we lived in Germany and they went there with their daughter and granddaughter. So they too settled in Chemnitz, but since Damberg was German, his family received an apartment rather than a single room, such as ours. We were glad to have our relatives nearby again.

My brother and I tried to continue our education in a German grammar school; since we did not know the German language, we were both placed in the first grade. We spent several months there, rapidly learning how to speak German until the start of 1945 when the Allied bombers abolished the city of Chemnitz. Before that, we were watching those bombers flying over our city to bomb Dresden, a large German city East of Chemnitz; we were thanking the Lord that we weren't their target.

But soon thereafter, the Allies, having annihilated Dresden, turned against us, and Chemnitz was bombed though not to smithereens at first. Our building was destroyed and we had to move in with the Dambergs, whose neighborhood was not heavily bombed and their apartment building stood intact. My brother's and my school were demolished, so we had no place to attend one. We didn't stay with the Dambergs for too long. Their building was located on a square with a park in the middle. It was a pretty neighborhood, though not for long. Several days after we moved there, there was an air raid alarm in the middle of night and we proceeded to the cellar as usual under such circumstances. Our valuables, food, and necessary equipment were already in the basement whose windows were covered with sacks of sand. There was water stored in barrels plus some bread and other food items, digging equipment, and other survival type items. And this time, much of that stuff was needed: the airplane. The noise was now accompanied with tremendous explosions. We were seriously bombed by the Allied B-25's and their British equivalents. The noise was unbearable even if you covered your ears, and when the bombing ended, I could not hear a thing. My hearing returned slowly, but for the rest of my life, my hearing was slowly declining until today, at the age of 85, I can't hear a thing without hearing aids. Our building was totally destroyed, but thanks to the German building methodology, the bombs did not penetrate the floors all the way to the basement and we were able to get out of there in the morning with our belongings that we kept in the basement. The outside world was a mess. Our building was a pile of bricks on top of the undamaged basement. All buildings that were standing were in flames, the park was pockmarked with wide bomb holes, in which the victim peoples made their camps. There were a few fire trucks around, but they could not do much. On the street, which was free of debris, there were bodies laying on the ground covered with tarps. We, the family, were all OK, thank God, and made a camp in the park with everyone else who stayed alive. Most faces, including ours, were black, covered with soot. In a few hours, we were all directed to walk outside the city where there was no bombing, and to a school, which was used as a "hotel" for a large group of bombed-out persons. We were allowed to spend a couple of nights there to receive directions where to go in Germany. Our family was directed to take the train to the Bavarian village of Neuenmarkt (near the city of Bayreuth, a place with yearly Wagnerian festivals), where we could rent a room in a farmhouse. Everything was organized so well by the German authorities under such awful conditions; it was a miracle! We were in a way lucky because we were directed to go to Bavaria, which was pretty far from the German province of Sachsen and its city of Chemnitz, which at the end of the war was occupied by Soviet troops. Bavaria was occupied by American troops.

Our trip to Neuenmarkt was reasonably normal considering what happened during wartime, such as attacks on trains by enemy airplanes, nothing happens on time, unexpected waits at stations or in the middle of wheat fields, etc. Our trip had an unforgettable occurrence, however, when at the rail station of Hof, a city in Germany's Frankenwald province where we had to change trains. There, someone stole my mother's portfolio that had all her documents and her money and jewelry in it. She was able to get a "foreigner's" passport from the German authorities, because my father had a copy of her Latvian passport (he had made copies of all our major documents before we left Latvia) and the German authorities thus didn't suspect anything funny. She used that German passport all the way into America until she received U.S. citizenship in the 1960's. But we eventually reached the Neuenmarkt village, where we settled in a room in a farmer's house as organized by the German authorities. In a few days we were joined in Neuenmarkt by the Damberg family; they too got a room in a neighboring farmhouse. It was winter, 1945, and the food situation was a bit scarce, but we and the Dambergs could acquire some food from the farmers with some gold items that we had brought with us from our former homes. Incidentally, the Dambergs' daughter Natalia had married a German air force pilot when they were still living in Posen. He was later killed on the Russian front and their daughter with her child was thus staying with them and traveled with them first to Chemnitz and then to Neuenmarkt. Living in a German village did not result in freedom from bombing. Neuenmarkt has a railroad station, and such transportation structures were always bombing targets which were often missed by bombs that, instead, were dropped on human habitats or barns. In our farmer's barn, a cow was killed by a bomb and bomb fragments flew all over the place. One of them penetrated our room's wall and destroyed my father's shaving equipment which he was using that morning (thanks be to God that it did not travel a few centimeters to the side and hit my father in the head). That bomb fragment flew into the opposite wall after destroying my father's shaving paraphernalia and fell on the floor. My father kept it with him for the rest of his life. But soon enough, at the end of the 1945 winter, the American tanks entered our village. Our German authorities expected their arrival and decided to defend the village. They forced the village males, including my father, to dig fox holes, and gave them rifles (I don't know what the German authorities expected the middle-aged riflemen to do against tanks with rifles). In the evening of the digging day, all went home to sleep and, in the morning, they were ready to occupy the fox holes to wait for the Americans. But all the fox holes were filled with water, which had seeped in at night. At that point, the elderly warriors gave up their rifles and went home. The Americans came into Neuenmarkt with their tanks without any trouble, and the peace of World War II followed shortly thereafter.

For one reason or another, our family decided to move from the American zone of Germany to the British one after the war ended, where our relatives, the Kijauskas' from Lithuania, were located. Mrs. Vera Kijauskas was my mother's sister and my godmother. She was married to a Lithuanian man by the name of John (we the kids called him uncle John. Also, he spoke perfect Russian) and they had a daughter named Eleanor, who was a year younger than my brother George (George was born in 1938). She now resides in Edmond, Oklahoma, but neither Uncle John nor his wife (my aunt Vera) are now with us. The Kijauskas were located in the Schleswig-Holstein's province, near the Danish border, in the village of Geschendorf, county Bad Segeberg, and they wanted us and the Dambergs to join them. We were always afraid of being deported back to Soviet Latvia by the Americans into the "welcoming" Communist arms. There were all kinds of rumors floating around about future deportations, and in fact, many former Soviet citizens were returned by the Americans to the USSR by force, and then sent to the Gulags for 10 years. But this did not apply to the Baltic people like us, which we did not know. The rumors were that the British did not do any forceful repatriations to the USSR, and mainly for that reason, our parents decided to move to the British zone, to join the Kijauskas family. Thus, the Bezkorovainys and Dambergs got on the train (its flat cars) and started the trip northward, to Schleswig-Holstein. But there was a problem: my mother had spilled boiling water on one of her feet, which scolded it heavily. It became infected on the way, and we had to put her in a hospital in a city called Lueneburg, located not far from Hamburg. This was a city where the parents of Natalia's deceased husband, her daughter's grandparents, were living. We stopped in that city; my mother went to a hospital, the Dambergs with their daughter and granddaughter stayed with their relatives, and my father, George and I slept in the railroad station. In due time, the German doctors cured my mother's foot and we could continue our journey. Natalia and her daughter stayed with their in-laws, but the Dambergs went northward with us. When we reached the city of Luebeck on the Baltic Sea, the Dambergs, having some acquaintances there, decided to remain there, and they lived there until the end of their lives. It was indeed a beautiful city... completely undamaged during World War II. For the rest of their lives, we kept in contact with the Dambergs, but we had never seen them again. And thus, we continued traveling northward until we reached the village of Geschendorf and the Kijauskas family. We stayed with them for a couple of weeks until we found a room for rent at a neighboring village called Weede, which was also in the county Bad Segeberg. We lived in Weede for half a year or so until all East European refugees from the Communist countries were collected into the so-called DP Camps, which were supported by the United Nations organization. DP stands for Displaced Persons.

And thus, in late 1945, we moved from Weede (with some intermediary stops) to the Rettberg Kaserne DP Camp in Eutin, Schleswig-Holstein province of West Germany, and remained there until May, 1951. It is said that before the Middle Ages, there were some Slavic tribes living in today's

Schleswig-Holstein area, and the term "Eutin" comes from the Slavic name "Utin," which comes from the word "utka." Translated into English, this means "duck." It is located on a relatively large lake, the "Eutiner See," and it has plenty of ducks throughout the area. Eutin also had a fairly large military garrison during the First and Second World War eras, and this group of fenced buildings was now converted into a camp for refugees from the Baltic countries: Estonians, Latvians, and Lithuanians. I understand that more than 10% of Latvia's population had left Latvia as the Soviets recaptured it from the Germans in 1944-1945. Like us, these folks were mostly professionals/intellectuals who feared Bolshevik atrocities that Russia had suffered after its revolution over the years after 1917, and the Baltic states had suffered, though not yet as heavily as Russia did, during Soviet rule from 1940 to 1941. I imagine that Estonia and Lithuania had also lost a similar percentage of its population; and it included the Kijauskas family, our relatives, whose family head, Uncle John, was a prominent Lithuanian businessman. Such DP camps existed for about 10 years, perhaps to around 1955, by which time most of the camp inhabitants were able to emigrate to various world democratic countries. The U.S.A., Canada, Australia, Brazil, and Argentina had agreed to accept them, including us. We left Germany for the U. S. in 1951, i.e., we stayed in Germany for some 6 years. The Kijauskas family left for America in 1949; Uncle John had some relatives in the U. S. and they helped his family to get there before many others could. We were also offered to go to the U. S. in 1949 because of my father's connection with a former Russian nobility organization, which, like relatives of the Kijauskas family, could sponsor the arrival of immigrants into the United States. Such sponsors, presumably, had a job ready for the sponsored immigrant family and an apartment ready for them where to live. For my father, there was presumably a job ready as a caretaker of an estate in Massachusetts, and there presumably was a house waiting for us on the estate premises. The Kijauskas family went to the U. S., and Uncle John got a job in a Chicago food factory and was able to rent an apartment to live in. But my father did not want to go; he had heard the job and living quarters promises were phony, that the immigrants, with the help of their sponsors, had to find jobs and places to live on their own when they got to the point of their destination in the U.S.A. So, he did not wish to face such an uncertainty in a strange country whose language, customs, and methodologies he didn't know. In other words, he was afraid that he couldn't make it in America; after all, he was already 50/years old. My mom was terribly upset. She told my father that next time, if we get another sponsorship to go to the U.S. and he refuses to go, she will then take the kids and leave Germany by herself. In two more years, we did receive another sponsorship, this time from YWCA in Wilkes-Barre, Pennsylvania, and we came to the U.S. in May, 1951, including my father. But we'll resume this particular part of our story below. The Eutin DP camp contained some 2500 inhabitants and was somewhat unusual as far as private families are concerned. We had a room in a former officers' quarters building, with common toilets and shower stalls. The camp had a "police" station with a jail, which was filled by young men who were formerly in the German army and became drunk and boisterous on weekends (since nobody had money, these folks were making their own spirits). They would break many windows in the corridors of the buildings where they lived. The glass had to be replaced with sheets of plexiglass, most of which could not be seen through, yet permitted the light to come in. They were let out of jail in a day or two when they would be sobered up. The camp inhabitants, with a few exceptions who were the camp "policemen," teachers, or office workers, were unemployed, and were fed and even clothed by U.N. organizations. After the war, practically all of Germany was unemployed, and it took the Marshall Plan and a few years to reverse that situation. So, we had common kitchens where we could get at least two meals a day. As pointed out above, the Eutin DP camp contained refugees from the Baltic Sea States, Latvia, Estonia, and Lithuania. Some 50% of its inhabitants were Latvians, the other two nationalities had 25% each. Over the years, the Baltic population was decreasing as families were emigrating for permanent lives in such countries as America, Australia, Argentina, Brazil and others, so that eventually there was enough room to bring in new refugees from Communist countries: we were joined by perhaps 1000 Serbs, refugees from Yugoslavia who were fleeing from their Communist regime. They were Orthodox, and with them was a priest and equipment to organize an Orthodox church. And this was a perfect gift for the few Orthodox members of the camp's Baltic peoples like ourselves. For all the camp's kids there were grammar schools for each nationality; my brother and I were attending the Latvian school, which had seven grades, like they had in Latvia. I started the 3rd grade at the end of 1945, and graduated from that grammar school in 1950. All my grades were 5's, i.e., top notch, and therefore I became the class valedictorian. The 1949 group had more students (all boys) than the 1950 group; half a dozen students had emigrated from Germany in that one year already since we had no high school in the camp, I had to go to the German one in the town, which was somewhat difficult to adapt to. In May of 1951, we emigrated to the United States, and I entered the sophomore grade at Coughlin High School in Wilkes-Barre, Pennsylvania. I finished high school with reasonable, but not perfect grades. We then moved to Chicago where I attended and graduated from Harrison High School in 1953 with a grade point rank average of No. 8 out of 300+ students. My brother George was 3 years behind me; he also was a graduate of Harrison High, but No. 2 ("salutatorian") out of 300+ graduates. Both of us then went to colleges, but that we'll describe below.

And so, let us return to the DP camp, where we stayed for 6 years. We the kids were busy going to school, even though there were few books, very little paper to write on, no gym items (our gyms were basically learning how to march like soldiers), and for music there was one broken piano and no other instruments. But we learned as best as we could, especially because we had excellent teachers, most of whose previous professions (in Latvia) were not school teaching. They were making a living in Latvia via other professions. A few examples: my Latvian language teacher (his name was Skuja or Skujinsh) was a Latvian poet and author. The one thing I remember about him is what he often said: "A person who is an author could write an entire novel about crossing a street, perhaps in Riga, but another normal person could not write a few sentences about his entire life." My mathematics teacher's last name was Perlbakhs (I forgot his first name), and he was an engineer in Latvia, who was telling us about planning bridges and other structures in Latvia. He was the best math teacher I ever had, even when I was taking calculus in college with engineering students when I was an undergraduate at the University of Illinois. His son was also a student in my Latvian class, and he also became an engineer and worked for the Boeing airplane factory in Seattle, Washington. He wrote me a nasty letter, because he had read my book "All was not lost," where I accused Russia's Latvian infantry regiments, the Strelnieki, organized during the First World War by the Russians to fight the Germans, to support the Communist revolution in Russia in 1917. In my opinion, they were the major military power to support the Communists; he disagreed with me... Well, "to each his own," as the saying goes. Our history teacher was Mr. Obrams (I forget his first name); in Latvia, he was a lawyer. He was always clear and concise, exactly how a lawyer would give a speech at the end of his client's trial. He was also our school's principal. Another Latvian teacher, whose name I've forgotten, was teaching biology and chemistry. He was an agronomist in Latvia, and he was telling us about fertilizers and crops, but in his chemistry class, I could never understand how to balance chemical equations. Eventually, at Harrison High in Chicago, I learned that there was no "rule" for that: you did it by "inspection"! Thus, everything about chemistry became so simple and clear that I decided to major in it in college.

In addition to going to school, I was a member of the Latvian boy-scout group that some experienced scout leaders in the camp had organized, and the time I did not spend in school or doing homework, I spent with boy-scout activities. It was a busy scout group under the leadership of our scout masters; in summer, we had camps in neighboring forests, and since our group was called "sea scouts," we had boats in the lake where we learned how to handle such items like oars and sails. The camps I did not like too much, since I was always cold when trying to sleep at night in the tents. I only had a blanket with me and no sleeping bag like some of my colleagues had and were thus much more comfortable at night. Nevertheless, the scouting situation was a lot of fun, and I often remember it very fondly.

My mom was trying to earn some Deutschmarks (German money) by opening a beauty "salon" in our room, which consisted of a chair and a standing hair dryer which she acquired for a few marks somewhere. And so, for a German mark or two, she would fix up her clients' hairdos, and both were happy with the outcomes: the client had got a professional hair job done and the beautician (Friseuse in German) got a few marks. Mom's Latvian license/diploma was sufficient to run such a salon and the money paid for extra food. I don't remember if she had to pay income tax to the German government.

As I pointed out above, my father refused to go to the U.S. when he had an invitation to do so from an association of the Russian nobility. In 1950, we received an invitation to go to Wilkes-Barre, Pennsylvania by its local YWCA, God bless them! I already pointed out above how my mother threatened my father to go to America with the kids by herself if he refused to accept another invitation. He had no choice, and we initiated the procedure to leave Germany. We did, and so in April of 1951 we got on a U.S. naval transport ship, the "General Stewart" and sailed to America. In New York, there was another examination of documents and my mother's X-ray pictures showed a fulminating TB disease, which was a big surprise. We were sent to Ellis Island instead of being released to go to Wilkes-Barre. After about a week on Ellis Island, which was a friendly and comfortable place, the authorities found no TB in my mother's lungs, she was perfectly healthy, and someone had apparently exchanged her lung X Ray image for a sick person's one so he or she could get into the U.S. without difficulty. So, we were let go, got on a train, and rode to Wilkes-Barre, Pennsylvania. There was of course no job waiting for my father or mother, and no apartment. We were taken by the YWCA folks to a former YMCA hotel, which still had furnished rooms with a bathroom ready for rent, and all necessary facilities to live in. We were told that we could stay there free as long as we wanted to, until our parents could get jobs and could rent our own apartment. The YWCA folks were also helping us to find jobs for my parents. Fair enough! My mom was soon hired by a clothing sewing company, and my father was offered a job in a steel mill; he could not stand the hot conditions there, and had to refuse to work there. He wasn't successful in finding another job. Meanwhile, my brother and I were going to school, and finished the current academic year in June, 1951 as indicated above. Wilkes-Barre was a nice town; we liked it a lot and would have been glad to stay there forever. There was a large Orthodox Church that we attended on Sundays, and the priest was very friendly and helpful with many things. But dad could not find a job, and the Kijauskas family in Chicago was inviting us to go there, since there were plenty of jobs in Chicago, they said. And that we did in summer of 1951 via a Greyhound bus, where mom, of course, got sea sick like she was on a ship traveling to America. We stayed with the Kijauskas family, and began looking for jobs for both mother and dad. Very soon both were working, and we had rented an apartment for $35/month in a house owned by a member of an Orthodox church to which we joined. Father became a janitor at the Combustion Engineering Company factory, where he remained over 10 years until his company moved to another city and let him go when he was 60 years old. He could never find another job (even with my help) and retired with a Social Security pension at the age of 62. My mom was working at a downtown restaurant making sandwiches, then in a factory making cardboard boxes, and finally went to a beauty culture school to learn all the modern techniques that had replaced the methodologies she knew from her experience with the Riga salon. She then passed the state exam, and worked in various beauty salons until her retirement, perhaps at the age of 75. My dad died in the year of 1975 at the age of 76. Mom died in 1988. Both were buried in the Orthodox section of the Elmwood Cemetery in the Chicago area.

As indicated above, I graduated from Harrison High in 1953 and entered into the 2-year Chicago branch of University of Illinois. In the early 1950's,

University of Illinois in Chicago was not what it is today: a 25,000-student institution that has all kinds of faculties, including engineering, and it grants Ph. D.'s in many areas, almost as many as those in Champaign-Urbana. In 1953, two years after my entry into it, it was basically a junior college organized to take care of World War II veterans, who, after serving in the armed forces, wanted to get an education. There were a huge number of them so that the existing state universities could not take all such qualified applicants. And a huge number of them were from Chicago. And so, the University of Illinois had established a 2-year branch in Chicago, apparently expecting that most (?) of them would flunk out during the first two years, so that the rest could be taken care of by the extant 4-year universities, including the big one in Champaign-Urbana. But eventually there were fewer than expected flunk outs and the public demanded that a 4-year state university be established in Chicago. And it happened, as I recall, in the 1960's, too late for me or my brother to take advantage of that. So at the end of 1955, when I did not have enough money to transfer and stay another 2 years at the University of Illinois in Champaign-Urbana, I had to transfer to another university in Chicago to get a degree. And so, I entered the University of Chicago in September, 1955, whose tuition was $230/quarter, and according to my calculations, I could get a BS in Biochemistry in additional 4 quarters, i.e., at the end of Summer, 1956 for a total of $920 tuition money. I could live with my parents, and earn $920 via part time jobs. And this is what I did, and graduated in the fall of 1956 with a BS in biochemistry; In the same year, my brother and I both became U. S. citizens. What to do next? My father wanted me to go to medical school; he didn't know much about what is involved to get into an American medical school (neither did I, for that matter). So I applied for admission to University of Illinois, which was (and is) in Chicago. I did not apply to any other of the 5 Chicago medical schools; their tuition were incredibly high (even then in the 1950's), and I didn't have the means to manage any of them. At my interview for admission to the University of Illinois Medical College, I was asked what I wanted to do as a doctor. As a typical University of Chicago student, I said that I wanted to do research to cure cancer. The interviewer said that he would not recommend my admission because the University of Illinois wants to train doctors who would practice medicine in rural areas of Illinois, especially in its southern counties, where there was a terrible doctor shortage. Then he said that I should get a Ph. D. in biochemistry (which was my major at University of Chicago), and that the University of Illinois in Chicago has a graduate college, where students can earn their Ph. D. degrees in biochemistry, anatomy, physiology, and other basic medical sciences (I did not know this). If I wanted to do cancer or other medical research, I should get a Ph. D. in biochemistry, my undergraduate major, he said. Then he said he would call the medical school's biochemistry department chairman and recommend my admission to their program. So what I, the neophyte, could do otherwise? Without any further issues or efforts, I was admitted to the University of Illinois in Chicago Graduate College Biochemistry Department to do their Ph.D. program work; my tuition was free(!), and I got an assistantship of $2000 per year, for which I had to help teaching biochemistry to medical students. Thus teaching biochemistry to medical students has become my employment for the rest of my life.

In September of 1960, after I finished my studies for the Ph. D. degree, I loaded my 1953 Hudson automobile with my belongings and drove to Oak Ridge, Tennessee to start working at my post-doctoral position at the Oak Ridge National Laboratory, Biology Division. My salary there was $6600 per year, which was enough for me to live on and send money to my parents, since my dad, at the age of 60, lost his janitor's job in his factory because they decided to leave the city. My mom meanwhile had passed the appropriate exams to become a licensed beautician, but her salary at her job was minimal. So I had to help them until my dad turned 62 years old and was able to receive his Social Security pension. I stayed at the Oak Ridge Laboratory for a year as per my contract with them. Life in Oakridge was the first time that I had to live alone. I rented a single room apartment for $55/month, I had to feed myself, do my own laundry, etc. Most of it wasn't a big deal except preparing food for dinner. On the first evening of my habitation, I decided to cook soup for dinner, which I did according to some cookbook directions; with some bread, it was tasty enough, and I went to bed. At night, I experienced massive diarrhea and serious pain in the belly, which forced me to stay at home for a whole week. After that, I never cooked my own dinner, and ate simple sandwiches for breakfast and lunch. For dinner, the main meal of the day, I ate at a restaurant across the street from my home, usually with my colleague from Norway, Dr. Froholm, who had an apartment in the same building I did. Its cost was $1.25 plus a tip. As far as work is concerned, I was appointed to a postdoctoral fellow position to Dr. Dave Doherty, a good scientist and a wonderful human being. He suggested that I work on blood platelet chemistry. I tried, but could never get a sufficient amount of bovine blood platelets; it was impossible to get enough human blood there. I then worked on various properties of bovine plasma proteins, and he was happy enough when we were able to publish 4 papers on the work I did. The chief of our Biology Division, Dr. Alexander Hollander, was a very friendly chap; he had me translate all the Russian papers that concerned his interests, and probably because of that, he offered me a permanent position at Oak Ridge National Laboratory, Biology Division. I did not particularly like the U.S. South, and I thanked him for his invitation to stay, but said no.

After about a year I moved to Ames, Iowa to work at the newly established National Animal Disease Laboratory as a GS-12 chemist with a salary of $8900/year. It was a U.S. Civil Service position, and the laboratory was connected with the College of Veterinary Medicine of Iowa State University, also located in Ames. We, the basic scientists, were promised to be given faculty positions (non-salaried) with that College, but it didn't happen as long as I was there. Nobody knew if and when it might happen! The Iowa State University in the city of Ames is located about 310 miles west of Chicago, and you could go there back and forth quite easily on U. S. 30, which I was doing often to see my parents and my "girlfriend", Marilyn. One memorable trip included a departure of my Hudson car from my ownership to the junk yard, when on my trip back to Ames, at some small town across the Mississippi River, the engine of my Hudson committed suicide and I had to get a new car. After I got back to Ames (I don't remember how), I bought a 2-year-old Plymouth, which I drove for the next 4 years. I hated it and promised myself never to buy another Chrysler car! In Ames, I stayed for a year; I rented a room for $40/month from a local engineer working at the Iowa State Highways Department located also in Ames (probably connected to the University's Traffic Engineering Department). He had a cat that he let out at night to roam, but one night, the cat got into a fight with another cat right under my window (the noise was enormous), and I had to pour a container of cold water to break them up so I could get some sleep. After that, the cat did not like me too much! All in all, the life in Ames was peaceful, my boss, Dr. Roepke, now and then reminded me that I should get together with some veterinarian scientist to help him solve his problems, but no veterinarian bothered me and I could do my own thing. During that one year in Ames I was able to publish four research papers, all were about bovine plasma proteins, especially the thyroxine-binding one. And with the other four papers that I published at Oak Ridge National laboratory, I had a good record in case someone wanted to hire a young biochemist with a decent publications record.

Soon enough, I received such an offer from Rush-Presbyterian-St. Luke's Medical Center in Chicago, where my friend, Dr. Max Rafelson, had become chairman of their biochemistry department. There was talk about resurrecting the Rush Medical College (in the 19th century, it was considered to be the best medical school west of the Hudson River), which used to stand where our Hospital stood. Rush Medical College was organized in the 1830's and was functioning until the 1940's when for some reason it closed doors (perhaps World War II had something to do with it). Yet its library was left intact, legally the right to reopen it had not expired, and in the 1950's there was circulating in the U.S. a thought that we didn't have enough doctors here, and that several new medical schools should be established to solve the problem. And the Rush administration proceeded to do just that. Dr. Rafelson, a professor at the University of Illinois Medical School, was hired to run the Biochemistry Department, and to further improve the department to make it ready for a new medical school; and I happily accepted their job offer at \$9600/year and Assistant Professorship rank at University of Illinois Medical College located a block from Rush. I stayed there until my retirement in 2005 A. D.

Marriage of Ignaty Bezkorovainy and Olga Solovey-Pavlichenko
in 1930 at the Alexander Nevsky Church in Riga in 1930

The author's parents (circa 1970), Ignaty and Olga

2657 West 15th Place Fist Bezkorovainy home
In Chicago, on the second floor.

Second Bezkorovainy home in Chicago at 1510 South Washtenaw
Ave.
Mom was 45 and George was 16.

Olga Bezkorovainy on steps of
1510 South Washtenaw Ave. at age of 50.

CHAPTER 2

FORTY PLUS YEARS OF LIFE IN CHICAGO

At this point, allow me to back up a little with my story of life in America. In Chapter 1, I wrote about our short life in Wilkes-Barre, Pennsylvania, and our move, in summer of 1951, to Chicago because my father could not get an appropriate job in our first stop in America. In Chicago, a 3-million population and number 3 city in the U.S., we were told, it was much easier to exist than in a small town like Wilkes-Barre, Pennsylvania, and we were not disappointed. Also, our relatives, the Kiajauskases, lived in Chicago for 2+ years when we arrived. And so, both my parents were working within a week of arrival, we, the teenagers, were attending schools (George in the 8th grade of grammar school and I in the Harrison High School's junior grade). We lived in a second floor of a 5-room (2 bedroom) apartment of a 2-storey building, which had a pizza parlor on the first floor the building was owned by a pre-World War I immigrant from Austria-Hungary's Slavic/Orthodox population (today, they would probably be called Ukrainians). He could speak some kind of Russian-Slavic dialect, so that my parents could converse with him (though I could not). He charged us only $35 per month's rent, God bless him! But life on his premises was not pleasant. First, the place was inundated by cockroaches. We had never encountered them in Europe, no matter how primitive our lives were sometimes. But here; their center of existence was the pizza parlor downstairs, and there was no way to get rid of them no matter what you sprayed around the place: The second problem was more serious: the pizza parlor was the hang-out of a city's teenagers' hooligan gang. They were always unhappy when they had to move from sitting on our steps leading to the stairs to our apartment, the glass of our windows was broken often, and there were shots fired from the street into our windows now and then. We, of course, went to the police to complain; in Europe, the police would have taken care of such disorders, but not in America, especially Chicago. The police said they could not do anything; just move, they said. Well, moving for my father was an activity of great horror. In Europe, we were always the last ones to move away from dangerous happenings, e.g., to move from Riga to Germany. The ship on which we sailed from Riga to Danzig was next to last that carried non-military personnel from Riga, or so I heard. And we were almost among the last DP's that left-Germany to the United States on a ship. Just take a look at the photos in chapter 1 of this book: the 1949 photo of my class had some 10 students more than the 1950's one. The missing students had already moved away to the U.S. or other countries from our DP camp, but we stayed around another 1-2 years to do so. So my dad waited and waited until it was impossible to live peacefully at 1534 West 15th Place, and then had us move just 1/2 block away tac' much nicer quarters (1510 So. Washtenaw Ave.), with perhaps a $10 per month higher rent. And I heard later that one of our former hooligan teenagers (from our former quarters, whom I knew) had shot some other kid to death and was thus sentenced to a long jail term. The new landlady of my parents' new apartment was a nice Austrian/German immigrant, who lived with her adult son on the first floor of our "new" 2-storey building. She, of course, spoke perfect German, which was a welcome gift for my mother who also spoke good German. So the two of them became good friends. My parents lived there for a long time, until the landlady passed away and her son decided to sell the building. There was a very willing buyer, the Mt. Sinai Hospital, which wanted to expand, and the house in 1510 So. Washtenaw Ave. had to be torn down to allow it. My parents, of course, were not ready to move for a long time (my brother and I no longer lived there). The new owners even threatened to turn off the electric current. But my father finally found an apartment on 24th Place near Washtenaw Ave. that he liked, basically in the same neighborhood as our previous one, and finally moved there with my mother. Mt. Sinai Hospital could then demolish our old building and build something new in its place. And thus the 24th Place apartment was where I moved in 1962 with my 1960 Plymouth car from Ames, Iowa back to Chicago, Illinois, where I remained living and paying a nice rent to my parents until June 8, 1964. On that Sunday, I married Marilyn Grib and we moved to our apartment at 7330 North Ridge Ave., close to the Evanston border, but I am getting a bit too far ahead with my story.

So, the year of 1962 was an important one: I moved back to Chicago to stay there all the years until 2005, my brother graduated from the University of Illinois with a B.S. degree in civil engineering in 1962, and my friend Marilyn Grib graduated from her teachers' college with a B.A. degree in elementary education. George stayed at University of Illinois to earn an

M.S. degree in traffic engineering (which took him another 2 years), whereas Marilyn got a job at a Morton Grove (a suburb of Chicago) elementary school third grade as a teacher. She invited me to attend her graduation ceremony, but I excused myself because George wanted me to attend his ceremony as well, which was to happen at the same date and time. The dear girl did not get mad at me for which I was quite thankful. Figure 2-1 shows Marilyn in her graduation garb.

So Marilyn and I saw each other quite often for over a year after I got back to Chicago, and I believe that somewhere in October, 1963 I proposed marriage to her. I was already 28 and I didn't want to get married like my father did, at an age of over 30. And I was very fond of Marilyn with whom I believed I could spend the rest of my life. So I proposed marriage to her and she accepted, but she wanted me to wait until June, 1964, whereas I thought that in a couple of days or weeks would be just fine. It was something about June that Marilyn liked; I couldn't figure out why, perhaps she wanted to finish the school year at her job as a teacher? But I agreed. And the marriage ceremony took place on June 8, 1964 with Archbishop John Garklavs of Holy Trinity Cathedral officiating. Holy Trinity Cathedral was Chicago's oldest Orthodox church, built around 1903, whereas the parish was established in 1892. Louis Sullivan was the architect who used the structures of the Siberian Railroad station churches as the style that he chose for the Chicago church. When he saw the built product, he was so impressed that he refused to take the money that the Trinity parish promised to pay him. The Russian Tsar Nicholas II paid about half of the costs to build the church (the total costs were about $30,000). And so Marilyn and I were married in a Russian Orthodox Church with already some history. It had been the church of Marilyn's family as long as they lived in Chicago, whereas mine and my parents' church was the Holy Virgin Protection Church (Pokrov in Russian), also Orthodox, organized in 1950 by the post World War II Russian immigrants to America. It is now located in Des Plaines, Illinois, a Chicago suburb. Since both are Orthodox churches, there were no disagreements or protests by anyone about our marriage. In fact, the priest who married us was Archbishop John Garklavs, who until November, 1944 was the Bishop of the Latvian Orthodox Church in Riga, Latvia and who left Latvia just about a month or two later than we did because of the common anti-religious persecutions of the Bolsheviks, who were pushing the Germans out of Latvia during World War II. Archbishop John's photo is shown in fig. 2-2.

Some few years later, both Marilyn and I became members of his church, the Holy Trinity in Chicago fig 2-3 but right after our marriage, we were still attending the Holy Virgin Protection Church, where my parents and I were members. Our son No. 1 Gregory was baptized there in 1965. As time went on, we moved for some reason to Holy Trinity (where we were married), so that our son No. 2, Alexander, born in 1969, was baptized there in the same year. And basically, from that time, we remained parishioners of the Holy Trinity Cathedral, where I was doing a few jobs for that (our} church: for a little while, I was its "starosta," for many years I was the treasurer/bookkeeper (I learned bookkeeping in law school), I was an organizer of several major festivals, and an author of its parish's 100th (1892-1992) anniversary book, which I will mention below. But let me explain the Orthodox church situation in America.

All Orthodox churches in America are separated on the basis of their parishioner nationalities (except in Alaska, there is no "American Orthodox Church," though the OCA is becoming one), which are controlled spiritually by foreign patriarchs or metropolitans and speak the same language, but whose members live throughout the area's geography which in case of Chicago is huge. The largest one in the U.S. (about 2.5 million members) is the Greek Orthodox Church, which has numerous parishes and large church buildings that cost millions of dollars to build. The Greeks are generally very successful business persons, and their richest American individuals are united into the "archon" organization, which basically runs their Orthodox church (some folks may disagree with that statement, but "to each his own"). Officially, the Greek-American Church is under the spiritual leadership of the Patriarch of Constantinople (today's Turkish city of Istanbul), who, with some difficulty, is currently trying to manage the American church's financial issues. The other Orthodox churches are much smaller. The more important ones among them are the Serbian Orthodox Church under the Serbian patriarchate, and two Russian Orthodox church organizations, The Russian Orthodox Church Outside Russia (ROCOR) and the American Orthodox Church (the OCA). The latter was organized when the Russians occupied Alaska in the 18th century. Their capital city was Sitka where the cathedral was located with the Archbishop's seat. The Alaskan church was very successful in converting many Alaskan natives into the Orthodox faith (from a pagan faith), the reason for which was a successful translation of service- and other Christian books from Church-Slavonic to the Indian dialects by Russian clergymen. The Orthodox Church is still very active in Alaska, which also has an Orthodox seminary to train priests for Alaska's native population. After Alaska was sold to the U.S. by Russia, the seat of the Alaska's bishop was moved to San Francisco to be in charge of Orthodox presence in the entire United States (later, another Russian bishop was appointed to handle strictly Alaskan Orthodox Christians). Because most if not all Orthodox immigrants entering the United States were settling in its eastern states, the seat of the Orthodox bishop was moved eastward to New York. Of course, now, the American Orthodox Church (OCA) is independent (autocephalous) since the Bolshevik revolution in 1917, and has its chief (Metropolitan) entity located in Washington, D.C.; there are several OCA bishops in various other American cities including Chicago and San Francisco. In most of its churches, the services are in English, though their leadership maintains excellent relations with the Moscow Patriarchate. The Russian Orthodox Church Outside Russia (ROCOR) was established in the 1920's in Europe by the Russian clergy who were evicted from Russia by the Bolsheviks. They expanded their presence in Europe, especially Serbia and France, where many Russian expatriates ended up. Very few of their churches were organized in America until the end of World War II, when the U.S. accepted a number of Russian immigrants who ended up in Germany feel like taking care of the yard any more. We bought a brand-new town-house with a 2 1/2 - car garage and 2 ½ baths in 1985, but we'll write about that later. And thus, we moved into our new living quarters in 1985 with only us 2 inhabitants, or so we thought. But, going back to 6801 N. Kilpatrick Ave., and the year of 1969, our son number 2 was born. This was probably an undesired event for Marilyn's mother, who refused to see her and our second son named Alexander (my grandfather's name) for a good six plus weeks. But it was just fine for me; now I had an opportunity to help take care of him and to get to know him well. He was baptized in the same year at the Holy Trinity Cathedral, which became our home church after we left the Holy Virgin Protection one. I don't remember exactly why; I believe it was because the services at Holy Virgin were all in Slavonic/Russian and Marilyn didn't understand the language, whereas at Holy Trinity they were in English (mostly). As far as I was concerned, I understood both languages, and for me there was no difference between the two of them.

And so, Marilyn was staying at home with the kids until Alex was in the second (?) grade of the Lincolnwood elementary school and Greg was in the sixth. At about that time, she got a job as an aide in a Skokie grammar school and in the evening, she took classes in the local teachers' college toward a Masters degree in special education. It took her between 2 and 3 years to finish that work, and she then got a job as the "principal" in a private Roman Catholic school for special children that was run by a very kind and helpful group of nuns. The school was located where their church was, in the same neighborhood near the intersection of Irving Park and Cicero Aves, not too far from where we lived. Marilyn liked very much to work there, though the pay was quite low, below $20,000/year with practically no benefits, and the real decision maker was not Marilyn, the "principal," but the cloister's chief nun. But Marilyn liked the place and its people and was happy to work there with the kids and the nuns. Happy, that is, until the chief priest of the convent got sick and died, and another one, with a totally different personality, took over. He didn't like nuns, and took over control of the school for himself, and it soon totally collapsed. Marilyn then went to work for the Chicago Board of Education at a regular city school on its West Side near the city's border with suburban Oak Park, which had a section for special education children. The pay was much better with some important benefits (Chicago schools are unionized), and she spent some 15 years there until she retired at the age of 62 in the year of 2000, when she decided to retire. I too retired from full time work in the same year (I was 65), though I continued working "part time" at two colleges for another 5 years.

Let me now back up a bit to pick up the second life that I had to lead beyond my life with Marilyn: namely, my life with my profession. My job at Rush-Presbyterian-St. Luke's Medical Center in the 1960's was going well enough. I was getting grants from the National Institutes of Health to do research in protein chemistry and iron metabolism, I was supervising some blood and other biological fluid chemical tests done by our department's medical technology laboratory, and I was teaching graduate students at the University of Illinois graduate school. In fact, I had some Illinois' graduate students doing their dissertation research for their Ph. D. degrees in my laboratory, since I had the title of Assistant Professor at Illinois. In the late 1960's, my employer decided to reopen the Rush Medical College, which functioned from the 1830's to mid-World War II, when for some unexplained reason, it closed its doors. Yet the library and license to function remained. We, the basic scientists, were pleased to get our own medical school to run and thus assume our teaching duties at our new medical school. But the hospital leadership, the MD's, decided that the new Rush Medical College will be a 3-year school (as opposed to all other U.S. medical schools which award the M. D. degree after 4 years of schooling). This would avoid the hire of basic scientists to teach such subjects as physiology, biochemistry, pharmacology, histology, anatomy, etc. These MD's decided that such subjects are useless for the practice of medicine (I thought that if this was so, we then might as well give the M. D. degrees to the nursing college graduates and let them practice medicine). This would save money, the Rush leadership claimed, because basic scientists like me would no longer be needed and they could dismiss me and the others like me and save money. As a result, I decided to acquire another profession so I could support my family if Rush let me go, and this turned out to be law, since I could go to a law school in the evening and still make a living to support my family during the day. I was accepted at several Chicago law schools and chose the IIT-Chicago Kent Law School, since it had the cheapest tuition. I spent four years there going to classes from 6 P. M. to 9 P. M. four days a week. Those were long days. In the morning, I would take a bus from our house in Lincolnwood to an Elevated Train station, where I caught a train to downtown Chicago, and then transferred to another train to go to the Medical Center. At 5 P. M. I took a bus to downtown Chicago where the law school was located and attended classes until about 9 o'clock, when I hurried to the Union Station to take a train to Lincolnwood (a 25-minute ride}. Marilyn and the kids met me at the station with our car. We sometimes would stop at a restaurant for dinner, but much of the time we drove home to put the kids to bed. This we did for 4 years until I graduated with a J. D. in 1977, passed my bar exam, and got a license to practice law. I was ready to open an attorney office, if I wanted to. One of my colleagues from Rush, a pharmacologist, did the same thing, and became a successful lawyer. But I did not quit Rush right away and waited to see what would happen. And what happened was that our medical students were flunking their national mid-term board exams en masse; such exams tested mostly basic medical sciences which our 3-year school omitted from its curriculum. Our school administration returned the curriculum to the normal 4-years and 95% of our students were then passing their national exams at the first try. Thus, my job remained safe and I did not have to go out and practice law for a living, but I still practiced it on a part-time basis for my friends and relatives; for instance, Marilyn's parents decided that they wanted to move to live in Florida. They bought a house there, in a town called Boca Raton, located on the shore of the Atlantic Ocean between Fort Lauderdale on the South and Palm Springs in the North. They sold their apartment building in Chicago on the shore of Lake Michigan, and I did all the legal work involved for them (no fee). And for my other friends and relatives, I helped buy and sell houses, write wills and contracts, and go to traffic courts to help them with traffic tickets (I didn't lose a single case). And all that I was able to do in my "free time."

So when the Rush administration decided that basic sciences were important to teach to medical students and my job was secure, I was promoted to full professorship and Associate Chairmanship by my boss Dr. Klaus Kuettner; he put me in charge of all departmental academic activities, including headship of our new graduate program which granted M. S. and Ph. D. degrees in biochemistry to graduate students. The "Rush Graduate Program "was established at Rush along with the medical school, although it had to be financed with grants awarded for doing research mostly by the Federal Government. It was approved by the appropriate State of Illinois administration. My boss, chairman of the Biochemistry Department Dr. Klaus Kuettner, was an expert of the connective tissue biochemistry and usually had large federal and private grants. He had a number of graduate students and postdoctoral fellows, and he hired half of a dozen additional faculty members for the Biochemistry Department, not to teach medical students which I was doing with an assistant, but to do research on connective tissue and teach his graduate students. These folks developed several graduate student courses on connective tissue chemistry and biology, creating a nationally important center of research in this area. I developed a course in "Science and the Law," which I gave every other year to graduate students. Two of them actually got so interested that they went to law schools, and are most likely doing work in patent laws or similar topics today. I should add that with the establishment of a medical school and a graduate college, Rush ceased to associate itself with University of Illinois academically, though it wasn't prohibited to be on Illinois' faculty if someone wanted to be. But now we had our own academic institution that had the right to grant university-level degrees.

As noted above, Marilyn's parents moved "lock, stock, and barrel" to Boca Raton, Florida. We used to visit them in Florida at Christmas time, usually staying there for 2 to 3 weeks depending on when our classes started in the new year, and perhaps also in summers, but when the kids got older, they were terribly bored to be all day with relatives, and so we decided to buy a condo located on a golf course where they could spend time playing golf. We usually rented it out for half a year after the New Year's festivities, with the rental income basically taking care of the loan payments. We even thought that we might retire there, but that didn't happen. Eventually the kids got older and did not wish to go with us to visit grandparents in Florida for 2-3 weeks at a time, and then something happened that forced us to sell the condo: we rented it for the usual 6 months to a young good-looking lady, who apparently had quite a few raucous parties that caused complaints from neighbors and did damages to the apartment. It cost quite a few bucks to repair it. We then sold it with quite a loss both with a good profit for the repair man and the IRS but not for us. But we continued to visit Marilyn's parents, staying with them until her father Nicholas, who was over 100 years old, passed away, and was buried in Chicago's Elmwood Cemetery. This was in 1998, or thereabouts, and Marilyn's mother then moved back to live in Chicago. Before Nicholas passed away, they already planned to return to Chicago because they could no longer manage their lives without help and had bought a condo on the shore of Lake Michigan in Chicago. Nicholas never made it back to Chicago alive, but Paula, Marilyn's mother, did. Yet being almost 90 years old, she was not able to lead a life on her own alone, and we took her to live with us in our townhouse in Lincolnwood. Ten years before that, we had my mother living with us as well when she was on dialysis and was totally unable to manage her own life. She had passed away in 1988; and now, at the end of the century, we had Marilyn's mother living with us, though she was not on dialysis. She was worsening mentally rapidly, and the doctors told us that she should be living in a nursing home since both Marilyn and I were working during the day and unable to control what she was doing at that time. In fact, several times when we were away, she had gone out "for a walk" outside the house and could not find her way back. Luckily, the police had picked her up and brought her home. She passed away in her nursing home on a Christmas day in the very late 1990's while we were visiting Alex and his wife in Arizona.

But getting back to our church lives, I was elected oy the Holy Trinity parish into several positions, one of which was the job of "starosta," the best translation of which may the "elder," or the parish president. This is not exactly like a corporate-type president, but one could translate it to something like the "elder," elected by the church's parishioners (in our churches, for one year). In addition to the "elder," the parishioners elect the church council, also for a year, which makes all non-spiritual decisions and is led by the starosta. The council usually has 12 members. So in one year, in the 1980's, I was elected starosta. One day, our church was expecting a group of visitors-clergymen from the USSR ranking from deacons to archbishops. There was some kind of international conference of religious authorities, and the USSR was, surprisingly, participating. And they wanted to serve in the Chicago OCA (Orthodox Church of America) cathedral. The OCA originated in Alaska when Alaska still belonged to Russia and which pronounced its independence after the Bolshevik revolution in Russia. But our clerical leadership had no problem with inviting members of its mother- and much suffering church to participate in common services with its members. But Chicago's Ukrainians didn't think that way. Their people began gathering around our church for 2 hours before the start of the service; and there were clergymen in full-service vestments outside the church waiting for the bus with the Russian clergymen. I found out that they were Uniates, not Orthodox, that is, Roman Catholics that use Orthodox vestments and services, but are Papists in regard to their basic beliefs. The Soviets actually outlawed the Uniate Church in the Soviet Union. I was told by those who knew Ukrainians that there were no Ukrainian Orthodox demonstrator priests among the mob of protesters. I was afraid that this mob may become violent when the Russian clergy would arrive and called the police to send some observers. The police refused, and we had to handle the situation however we could. We helped the Russian clergy to enter the church with all the yelling, whistling, and swearing by the mob, but they did not touch anyone and after the service started, most disappeared. Some actually came into the church and stayed for the service without bothering anyone. I approached a Ukrainian woman whom I saw outside yelling obscenities at the Russian clergy and asked her what she was doing inside the church. She responded that this was a free country and she could be wherever she wanted to. C'est la vie! When the service ended, there was no problem with the Russians having a cup of coffee in our hall next door, and entry into the bus to take them back to their hotel. When some 20 years later I was in Tikhvin, Russia accompanying the return of the Mother of God icon written by St. Luke to Russia from America, I met there with a deacon who had been in Chicago in the 1980's with the Russian group. I asked him how he felt about it. And he said that he was quite afraid that the Ukrainians would become violent, but was glad that nothing beyond yelling obscenities took place. I apologized to him for the behavior of my countrymen! Some other unusual event occurred to me as well during my one-year job as "startosta." The situation that developed involved a weekly publication of church news by our church. The bulletin had four relatively small pages, with an icon on the front page and 2 ½ pages where the church could print other information. Usually, our priest printed the service schedule there and some other news, leaving some space blank. I thought that this weekly publication could be an excellent method to teach some essentials of the Orthodox faith to the parishioners. To start with, I decided to print the life of a saint in each Sunday's bulletin. This did not push out any other information that was being printed in this weekly bulletin. I did a couple to these, when Father Sergey told me to stop it. I told him that being a teacher, I thought it might be a good idea to educate our parishioners about the lives of our saints, since every week there was blank space left for it and nothing had to be omitted. He said that this was a job for him to do and not for me, and that I should cease and desist. I waited for him for a while to start doing it but he never did. I then told him that I wish to resign from my starosta job because he obviously did not trust me. He asked me to stay until next year's election and I did. But no one continued doing what I had started to do. Yet after all this, I was elected bookkeeper and treasurer of the parish many times, and the priest never protested any of it. Father Sergey retired and passed away a few years ago. God bless his soul, but I am still wondering why he stopped my attempt to honor the saints.

During the years of my membership at the Holy Trinity Cathedral of Chicago, there were two events whose celebration were of great importance to the parish and for the celebrations of which I had a rather large participation and control: the 1000-years of Orthodoxy in Russia (from 988 A. D. to 1988.A. D.) and 100 years of existence of the Holy Trinity Orthodox parish in Chicago in 1992. Preparations for these events took a long time, of course, and the planning had to start almost a year before the event had to take place. The celebration of the 1000th year of Russian Orthodoxy was suggested by Gordana Trbuhovich and myself at a Holy Trinity council meeting. We presented our ideas about doing this at a church council meeting and the starosta (I think it was Steve Smarsh at that time) took a vote after a discussion. The votes were 7 Ayes and 5 Nays, and Bishop Boris, who was present at the meeting, announced that he will think about it and will give his decision at the next monthly meeting. Bishop Boris was a strange person; a retired former U.S. Navy chaplain with a rank of Lieutenant Commander (as I remember) and son of Austro-Hungarian immigrants to the U.S. (and like most of them, former members of the Uniate/Roman Catholic church). We weren't certain what kind of decision Bishop Boris would pronounce, but he said to go ahead, God bless him! And ahead we went; it turned out to be a great event on Saturday and Sunday of September 3 and 4, 1988, 1000 years after Kievan Rus became officially an Orthodox country. Figure 2-Summarizes the events. On September 3, we had a scholarly symposium on Russian and American connections with the Orthodox faith-events that were centuries apart. The Russian tribes led by "princes" (the Kniazi, most of whom were of Viking origins) were all pagans, but the most important and powerful one, the Prince of Kiev Vladimir, realized that those being "modern" times, pagan faiths were no longer logical or useful, and the people of Rus should become monotheists, like all their neighbors were. And there were many examples of such monotheistic countries, e.g., the neighboring Khazars had accepted the Hebrew faith, the Poles-Roman Catholic, the Tatars-Islam, and so forth. But when St. Vladimir sent his ambassadors to the Hagia Sophia church in Constantinople, they came back praising the Orthodox Christian service saying that they did not know if they were in heaven or on earth when they were there. And so, Prince Vladimir, who became a Saint Prince Vladimir eventually, ordered all Russians baptized into the Orthodox faith 1000 years before the year of 1988. And this date was so powerful in Russia that the Bolsheviks could not prohibit the Orthodox Church of Russia from celebrating this event. And it took less than half a dozen years after that for the Communist regime in Russia to collapse. On Saturday September 3, 1988, the Holy Trinity organized a scholastic symposium on the nature of the Orthodox faith at the St Mary of Nazareth Hospital auditorium (across the street from the Holy Trinity Cathedral). It took place with 7 speakers from 9 A.M. to 5 P.M., with 1 hour break for lunch, followed by a Vespers service, and ended by a social "cafe a la Rus." On the next day, a Sunday, there was a procession at 9 A.M. from the parking lot to Chicago Navy Pier's auditorium (on Lake Michigan) led by Archbishops of Chicago's Greek, Serbian, and Russian Orthodox Churches. In the harbor, there happened to be a visiting German warship, with all its sailors standing on its left side watching the procession (I was very happy that the ship did not overturn and sink). The liturgy was served, then a blessing of the lake waters with a floating large wreath of flowers was done, and a banquet was followed. At 5 o'clock, there was a concert by the Chicago Symphony Orchestra led by Dr. Peter Jermihov, and the feast was ended by a GALA BALL. On Michigan Ave. were hanging posters announcing the 1000th year festivities. In the vestibule of the Holy Trinity Cathedral was hung a monumental stone plaque (among other such remembrance items) in commemoration of the 1000-year event. I hope that it will last for another 1000 years with the building in which it is located.

I think that Bishop Boris liked the way the event preceded; very smoothly, no hindrances or problems, no complaints. He could be, and was, proud of what HIS church had accomplished. He gave a nice thank you plaque/gramata (paper) to Gordana Trbuhovich (she definitely deserved it), but gave nothing to me. And it wasn't just time and effort that I spent doing the work. We lost some money doing the job; by "we" I mean myself and Mr. Rostislav Diakon, a pharmacist (God bless his soul), whose father was the priest at OCA's St. George Church in Chicago. He and I made up the difference from our own pockets, so that the Holy Trinity ended up not spending anything for this event. But the big boss couldn't even give me a thank you gramata or to Mr. Diakon which we could put in frames and hang up on our home walls. I don't remember it, but I guess that I may have complained about this (privately, of course) to Archbishop Alipii Gammanovich (of the ROCOR Chicago diocese) at a conversation, who was our friend and was invited to, and did attend, our Navy Pier celebration (his church had its own much simpler celebration later in the year, which Marilyn and I attended). He reported this to his Metropolitan in New York (I don't know exactly why since it had nothing to do with him or his church), and they gave me a very beautiful gramata signed by their bishops with a thanks for my efforts even if my own bishop demurred. God bless Bishop Alipii's soul and grant the other bishops who signed the gramata many years. That gramata, in a nice frame, is now hanging in my Sun Lakes home. And speaking of Archbishop Alipii's memory, I must mention another thing that involved him: some couple of years before this Millennium event, I asked Archbishop Alipii, who was a superb icon writer, to write an icon for me privately commemorating the building of Holy Trinity Cathedral back in 1903. He agreed to do it for a very reasonable price. He did the job, a piece of wonderful work indeed showing the organizers of doing the building: Patriarch St. Tikhon, who was the Metropolitan in America when Holy Trinity was built and St. John Kochurov who was the priest in Chicago at that time, and who was the first priestly victim of Bolshevik atrocities in Russia. I had the icon hanging on the wall in my house. Now, when the Tikhvin icon of the Mother of God was being returned to Russia from Chicago in 2004 A. D., the Russian airplane that flew to Chicago to pick up the icon had the Metropolitan (God forgive me, but I forgot his name) of St. Petersburg on it to accept it. I got a call from Father John of the Holy Trinity Cathedral, our priest, that he wanted to give a gift to the St. Petersburg metropolitan, but he didn't know what to give. I don't know if he already had something in mind; it wasn't money and it must have been something that I had that no one else did. And it was most likely Archbishop Alipii's icon, though he didn't mention it specifically. I did, and he gladly agreed. And so, my Bishop Alipii's icon went to Russia along with the famous Tikhvin icon and is now, most likely, hanging in the St. Petersburg Metropolitan's office. I often think about it.

A similar but much simpler event took place in 1992 celebrating 100 years since the establishment of Holy Trinity parish/cathedral in Chicago (1892), Chicago's first Orthodox church. To celebrate this event, I was given the job to write the church's history book which we published in 1992 with the title of "History of Holy Trinity Russian Orthodox Cathedral," edited by me and containing the following articles: "Foreword," by His Beatitude Metropolitan Theodosius; "Preface" and "One hundred years of service to God and man" by me; "A cloud of witnesses," by Thomas E. Klocek; "Sacred song at Holy Trinity Cathedral" by Leonard Soroka, our choir director; "Iconography of Holy Trinity Cathedral," by Matushka Alexandra Garklavs; "The architecture of Holy Trinity Cathedral," by Charles Gregersen; and "The present and future state of Orthodoxy in America," by Roderick F. Mollison. The book was hard covered with a total of 146 pages and the size of 8 1/2 x 11 inches (ISBN 0-9632743-0-9). We had 1000 copies of it printed. As I recall, it was sold out rapidly at $30 each. Our church had a festive celebration on a Sunday on this occasion, at which time I was given a gramata by Metropolitan Theodosius, dated on June 14, 1992, with a thanks for its authorship.

In the next year, 1993, there was yet another celebration, in which I did not seriously participate, nor did our church, except for a regular service on that day. It was the 200th anniversary of the introduction of the Orthodox faith into America by Russia through its colony of Alaska in 1793. The Patriarch of Moscow/Russia's Aleksy II was in Chicago and participated in a service in Chicago's Arie Crown Theatre on September 25, 1993. This visit was probably arranged by the Greeks and basically all the Orthodox folks of Chicago (200,000 of them) were participants physically or spiritually. An icon was written to commemorate this event, which shows the saints associated with bringing the Orthodox faith to America from Russia and an Alaskan Indian boy among them who was captured by the California Spanish forces and demanded that he abandon the Orthodox faith and accept Catholicism. The boy refused and was killed by the Spanish. He was the first Orthodox martyr sainted in America. This 1993 event was well publicized in Chicago, where Mayor Richard M. Daley developed a "Proclamation" stating why this Orthodox festival was also a feast for the entire city of Chicago. Only the Greeks could force a Chicago mayor to do this, I am sure, and it might have cost them a fortune; but God bless them for doing such a great job!

So after our city was visited by the Russian patriarch in 1993, I was 58 years old; I was still doing my usual bookkeeping job for the church and the level of work in the Department of Biochemistry was increasing, yet my energy level was beginning to decline. So, I no longer was volunteering to do additional jobs for the church, since I believed that I had enough gramatas hanging on my house walls. And in 1994, I began traveling rather often to various places in our world, including Russia. It dropped communism in 1991, but I still didn't trust them to be normal with respect to tourists and unwelcome visitors. However, after I had contact with the patriarch in 1993 and other Russians that visited America, I decided that I'll try to go there to meet my relatives and see what is going on there. Marilyn and I went to Russia for the first time in 1994 with our church group, and we were not disappointed. Since then we have been in Russia perhaps a dozen times, seen my relatives, and visited the ancient holy places, many of which have been repaired and remodeled. And we didn't forget my birth place, Riga, Latvia (today, an independent country), and the building where we had our apartment on the fifth floor. It is now a condo building with a newly constructed elevator. Today's cost of our apartment-one million dollars!

One of the most memorable trips to Russia was with the return of the Tikhvin Mother of God icon to Russia in 2004. Written by Apostle St. Luke, the icon was kept in Constantinople until its conquest by the Turks, then it appeared in Russia (found by a peasant in a northern Russian forest) during the reign of Ivan the Terrible, who ordered a monastery built where the icon was found, and to keep the icon there. It was called the Tikhvin Monastery, Tikhvin being a neighboring town. That was done, and for hundreds of years pilgrims were coming to Tikhvin to venerate the icon. When the Bolsheviks came to power, they destroyed the monastery and put the icon in a museum.

During World War II, the Germans picked it up because its frame contained gold and jewels, but they did not take it to Germany for some reason and left it in Riga, Latvia, with its Orthodox bishop John Garklavs as its keepsake. He took it with him to Germany and then to America in 1949, where it was maintained by him at the Holy Trinity Cathedral of Chicago. The icon was there when Bishop John married Marilyn and me in 1964. When Communism fell and the Tikhvin Monastery was restored, the icon was returned to Russia in 2004 A.D. by Father Sergey Garklavs, an adopted son of Bishop John (Bishop John had already passed away). Marilyn and I accompanied the icon to Russia with several other Chicagoans, and witnessed its installation back in the Tikhvin Monastery's cathedral in the presence of an enormous crowd of people. The above story is a short version of one of many other trips that I have described in my previous book, "Beyond All Was Not Lost," published by Dorrance Press in 2020.

And so, in the year of 2005, Marilyn and I decided to move to Galena, Illinois. We were somewhat sorry to leave Chicago, but all our relatives were either dead (our parents) or moved away: Gregory was living in Brooklyn, New York and Alex and Nora in Arizona. Greg graduated from the University of Illinois in 1987 with a BA in English, and moved to New York, where, on part-time basis, he earned an MA degree in English from Hunter College. He works as a writer for a medical literature publishing firm, is married, and has 2 kids. Alex graduated from Illinois State University with a BA degree in history in 1993 and went to dePaul University to take courses in teaching of history. He passed the Illinois teachers' examination and was teaching history in a Chicago suburban school when he got married and moved to Chandler, Arizona, where he got a teaching job in a Phoenix area high school. Unfortunately, he became divorced from his wife whom he had married in Chicago, and he never married again. Both my and Marilyn's parents were deceased and buried in Chicago's Elmwood cemetery. My brother George, an engineer and 3 years younger than I, is living with his family in Massachusetts. And Marilyn's relatives, with whom she has few if any connections, live in various cities far away from Chicago. Thus, we have few if any relatives remaining in Chicago, and our move elsewhere has not been terribly tragic. We liked Galena very much; we have been there from time to time since the kids were very young: I have a photo with Alex (5 years old) and Greg (9 years old) standing next to an antique automobile at an antique car show in Galena in the year if 1974. They had at least one antique auto show every year. I still remember the show of Packard automobiles, which was most impressive. And as I had pointed out above, we had bought a 900 sq. foot cottage in the Galena Territory as an "escape" location around the year of 2000. So now we sold our cottage and bought a large house, some 3000 sq. feet in area on a ½ acre lot. It cost $260,000, and we moved there in 2005 "lock, stock, and barrel."

Galena is located about 180 miles from Chicago, in Northwestern Illinois, on the Mississippi River, across from Dubuque, Iowa. It is older than Chicago, and was at one time an important government and trade center at the beginning of the 19th century, before railroads were built. In fact, for a time, it was arguably the largest city in Illinois. Near Galena and across the river were lead mines that produced a large percentage of the bullets for the Union Army during the American Civil War. During that war, Galena produced seven Union generals, including the commander of all the Union Armies, Gen. Ulysses S. Grant. He was born in Galena where his father owned a leather goods store. He was a graduate of the West Point Academy, and participated in the U. 5.-Mexican War, then retired and worked in his father's store. He was drafted back into the Union army when the U.S. Civil War started, and he organized a Union infantry regiment from the Galena men which he commanded. He eventually became the leader of all Union armies and won the war for the United States. After the war, he was elected U.S. president twice. The city of Galena had built a large house for him and his family, hoping that he and his wife would come home to live, which he did, though only for a few months before he had to go to Washington to take over the U.S. presidency. He never returned. Today, his house is a national museum. On the left shore of the Galena River is a park in which stands a large monument, a statue of Ulysses S. Grant, a famous Galena citizen. The name is Grant Park.

As far as our spiritual lives are concerned, we found an Orthodox Church in the city of Dubuque, Iowa across the Mississippi River from Galena. It is the St. Elias Greek Orthodox Church which we attended for a couple years. But because of the politics going on there, we had to move away; in those couple of years, we became very friendly with the priests that served there. Father Golemis was an erudite person, who lived in Chicago and went to serve in Dubuque on Sundays and Feast Days. We often drove him back to Chicago on Sunday evenings when we were still living and working there and spent many weekends in Galena. Some church powers did not like him for some reason and had him replaced by Father Andoni Callozzo. He is of Italian descent, who became Orthodox when he was a teenager. He came to St. Elias when we were already living in Galena, and he settled to live in the church's house. The powers that be were constantly complaining to the bishop that Father Golemis lived in Chicago, and that was, in part, why he had been released from St. Elias. So Father Andoni should have been exactly what they wanted, or so we thought. For us, Father Andoni became a good friend and spiritual father. One reason was his gift to me of St. Anatoly's icon either on my birthday or name's day, which he himself had written (he was an accomplished iconographer). St. Anatoly was, like St. George, was a Roman soldier, and the two of them were friends, though only St. George was a Christian (which was illegal in Rome). St. George was sentenced to death, and St. Anatoly then pronounced himself to be a Christian as well. Both Christian friends were then tortured and executed (by the way, my brother's name is George, as in Russian tradition). Father Andoni wrote the Anatoly icon (fig. 2), and (years later) drew a picture of himself he sent to me for some reason. Thanks, Father Andoni; it fits nicely in the book. But to get back to our story, the church's archons wanted Father Andoni's dismissal, and the bishop did what they wanted: he released Fr. Andoni. He got another position in Youngstown, Ohio, and moved to live in the nearby Pittsburgh, Pennsylvania, where his relatives were living. Father Andoni had since then retired, and continues living in Pittsburgh, may the Lord bless him!

Marilyn and I left St. Elias joined St. Vladimir's parish, a ROCOR (Russian Orthodox Church Outside Russia) church located in a Russian settlement, Vladimirovo, near the city of Freeport, Illinois. It took us 1.5 hours on Sunday mornings to get there, but there were no "archons," or other "powers that be," and everyone was friendly and helpful. This "Vladimirovo" community was established in the 1970's basically by the ROCOR Archbishop Seraphim of Chicago, who wanted a countryside "Russian village," where retired Russian-Americans could settle and which could organize various summer activities, including a boy-girl scout camp, where kids could learn the elements of Russian culture and the Orthodox faith. This camp had attracted 100+ kids per year from all of the U.S. and lasted for over one month. Archbishop Seraphim had a small but pleasant church built there (St. Vladimir's Church), appointed a permanent priest, Father John Sikalyuk, who lived in the nearby city of Rockford, Illinois. He is a retired engineer from a Rockford industrial organization. The services were conducted in the Slavonic language, but the choir was somewhat primitive, led by an amateur, yet eager director. Exceptions were in summers, during the boy-girl scout camps, when the choir was led by Peter Jermihov of Chicago, who teaches music in a Chicago college and directs the choir of a large Greek Orthodox Church. He is a perfect Orthodox choir director, may God grant him many years! For us, this church was perfect, no problems, no fights, and I was even elected to be the church "treasurer," which really did not involve handling any money (as per my wish), but involved handling accounting books. I even got a "gramata" from Bishop Peter Lukianov for my efforts. The only "negative" in regard to the Vladimirovo church was its distance from where we lived in Galena; it took us 1.5 hours to drive there via 2-lane highways on Sunday mornings. But that was a minor issue, and we were very sorry to leave that parish when we had to move to Arizona in 2015. We sold our Galena house for $180,000, some $80,000 less than what we paid for it 10 years earlier. But it was enough to pay off the $115,000 debt that we owed for the house in Sun Lakes, plus for building an additional room to it. The living community was not strange to us, since we started coming to Sun Lakes some 5 years before 2015 to escape the northern winters. And our son Alex, as well as my cousin Nora, were living here, so we were not complete strangers here after all. Yet we did miss, and still do so, our former habitat in Galena of Northern Illinois.

And so, at this point I will start the story of our life in Sun Lakes, Arizona. In the fall of 2015, Marilyn and I got into our 2012 Honda CR-V car and started our drive toward Arizona. For me, it was a sad journey; I loved living in Galena, and was originally hoping to live there for the rest of my life. And it seemed that Marilyn was having the same kinds of thoughts. But now I was thinking whether or not I will ever see our town Galena ever again, as we drove westward from the Galena Territory, across the Galena River bridge, past the 19th century red brick buildings on U.S. 30 toward the Mississippi River and Dubuque, Iowa across it. The sad voyage lasted some 3+ days before we reached our new home in Sun Lakes, Arizona. On the way, we stayed 3 nights in motels along the road, since Marilyn was getting easily tired as her Parkinson's Disease had advanced for some 3 years already (she was diagnosed around the year of 2012). Normally (in the previous years) our trip took some 2 ½ days with 2 nights on the road, the second one being in Gallup, New Mexico, where we loved to stop and examine all those local Indian arts stores (our favorite one was owned by a Greek immigrant and not by an Indian). But this final time it took us 3 days to get there, to stay the night, and take another day to get to Sun Lakes. There, we already had a house, which we had for some 5 years and where we stayed for winters to get away from the Galena snow falls; we stayed there normally for about 5 months (end of November to mid-April). Only this time, we never expected to get back north.

The reason why we were spending our winters in Sun Lakes, and now moved there for permanent habitat, was for at least 2 things: our neurologist told us that they, in Dubuque, are not trained to handle Parkinson's Disease. We should go to expert doctors either at the University of Iowa in Iowa City, or to Rockford, Illinois (quite a distance for either town, especially in winter time). We thought that in such a case, we might as well return to Chicago, which we did not want to do. The second issue was that we had to sell our 2 ½ story house in Galena, since Marilyn could not climb its stairs any more. A suitable one-storey house we already had in Sun Lakes, Arizona, which would be hard to find in Galena. Our younger son Alexander was living in Chandler (Sun Lakes may be considered to be Chandler's "suburb"); he was (and is) teaching history in a local high school, which he had been doing for 15 years. Also, my aunt Vera and her daughter Nora with her husband were living nearby, in Scottsdale, before my aunt had passed away. Thus, the area was not foreign to us. And most importantly, we already had a suitable house there, so that it was not necessary to stay with relatives or in a hotel while searching for one. It was somewhat smaller than our place in Galena, area-wise some 1800-1900 square feet, built in the 1980's and with 3 bedrooms. Thus, it was smaller than our Galena house, and it was somewhat difficult to get used to that. The garage was especially small though it was designed to hold 2 cars (maybe for 2 Volkswagens?). We ended up with our garage half-filled with our items that didn't fit into our living quarters, e.g., we had to build an area of shelves from floor to ceiling, where our books were stacked, plus photo albums with pictures taken in much of the world in the prior 60 years. And my science books took a tremendous amount of room. With all such items, plus tools for painting and yard work, trunks, etc. in a 2-car garage, there was room only for one medium-sized car, which was our Honda CR-V. Otherwise, there were no steps in the house, no attic or basement, i.e. perfect for a family with a person in a wheelchair.

After we moved into our house at 25449 So. Truro Drive, Sun Lakes, AZ, we decided to add another room to it on top of the concrete floor that was located next to the rear part of the house, which also had a roof but no walls; it was like an open porch about 400 square feet in area. We decided to have walls constructed around it and thus add another room to the house. This veranda-like structure was built within one day and cost $25,000 for the work and materials. At each of the two ends were sliding glass doors and windows in between. In one window we installed an air conditioner that could maintain the temperature in the veranda at about 75 to 80 degrees F on hot summer days when the outside temperature was often over 100 degrees F. However, there was no heater in case the temperature would drop below freezing during wintertime. We put some furniture in that new room, but haven't used it much yet. Somehow, we still don't know what to do with that room yet, except when our grandchildren are in town and want to watch TV or play games without bothering anyone else.

Like we did with our house in Galena after we moved there in 2005, we did a number of repairs on our Sun Lakes house such as putting up a new roof (the old roof was the original one of the houses, which was leaking when it rained outside), installed vertical blinds on all glass doors, put on a new garage door... The air conditioning machinery located on the house's roof conked out and had to be replaced for $10,000; the refrigerator has been fixed already 3 times, our washing and drying machines had to be rehabbed twice, the garbage disposal-grinder had to be replaced twice, the list goes on... In addition, the yard requires maintenance "repairs" all the time. The house's previous owners liked fruit trees: when we got the house, there were 3 orange trees, a grapefruit tree, a lemon tree, several fir trees, and two "triple" palm trees. After our 10-year ownership, we have left one orange tree, one grapefruit tree, and a lemon tree, plus the palm trees. Every year something breaks down and must be fixed or replaced. In other words, "normal" events happen all the time, but the ones here seem to be more "normal" than what we have experienced before in Galena. In place of the trees that had died, we planted a bunch of rose, bushes and hired a garden maintenance company to handle our yard plants. They come once a month and it costs $80 for their assistance. So far, so good, except that the rose bushes are no longer producing the usual beautiful rose flowers. But at least none have yet died.

Sun Lakes, our community, is not an official city, town, or village. Yet it has some 23,000 residents, according to my calculations. It is located on the southern side of Chandler, and is simply a part of Maricopa County of Arizona. Yet it has its own fire department and emergency ambulance service. When I needed to take Marilyn to the Chandler hospital, the Sun Lakes ambulance and a fire truck were at the house within 5 minutes of my call. Compared to Galena, Illinois, this is a superb part of living here. In Galena, the fire department is based on volunteer services, whose arrival at a fire takes 30 to 60 minutes. Under such circumstances, all they can do in case of a fire is to prevent the fire from spreading to neighboring buildings. But the house on fire is usually a total loss. But the Sun Lakes community does not have its own police department; the police work is done by the Maricopa County sheriff's office, and they are pretty good at it. The housing neighborhoods are mostly behind guarded gates; you can't get in there without your I.D. card. The exceptions are the two town's initial housing units, Cottonwood and Sun Lakes Country Club. Though they are surrounded by concrete fencing, you can get in there via several through streets. These were the initial housing neighborhoods built in Sun Lakes; our house is located in the Cottonwood area and we have our own private patrol system here. In our five-year full-time occupation of our house, we haven't heard anything about crime increases here. But because we had already been questioned several times whether or not we want our community to become a haven for illegal South American immigrants (a la Chicago and other big cities), we have acquired an ADT alarm system for our house.

We moved to Arizona basically because of Marilyn's sickness, diagnosed by a Dubuque neurologist as Parkinson's disease. And he said that in Dubuque, Iowa they had no specialists who could best handle the disease. The nearest place to do so would be either Rockford, Illinois, where a University of Illinois medical school was located, or in Iowa City, where the University of Iowa Medical School was located. Both were over 100 miles from Galena. And to stay in Galena, we needed to get a new house with a single storey and no stairs to be able to handle a wheelchair. Such houses are very uncommon in Northern Illinois, but we had one in Sun Lakes, Arizona. And in Phoenix, Arizona there was the Mohamed Ali Institute designed to diagnose and treat Parkinson's Disease. And thus, we moved to Arizona "lock, stock, and barrel" in the fall of 2015 and registered to see an expert doctor at the Mohamed Ali Institute once a month. We were going there for 2 years. The Institute charged Marilyn's insurance company up to $600 per visit, but absolutely nothing was done or attempted to do to prevent the progression of her disease. Besides, as Marilyn's health and mobility declined, it was more and more difficult to get her organized and bring her with a wheelchair to the Institute to see its doctors. Dr. Ku, our general practitioner, suggested placing Marilyn into a diagnostic hospital of HealthSouth in Mesa, Arizona to determine what is basically going on and what can be done for Marilyn. She stayed there for 10 days, and their conclusion was basically that she had Parkinson's Disease and that nothing, other than care, can be done for her. This was in Spring of 2017, and we took her home. We then organized two services for Marilyn in order to keep her comfortable and look after her medical needs. One was a Hospice Family Care company, which provides medical/nursing care for patients at home, and the other, Home Care Assistance that provides 24/7 assistance for patients' maintenance at home. The Hospice Family Care sends a nurse (an RN) to see a patient twice a week, who measures the patient's vital signs, prescribes drugs, and performs various procedures, i.e., provides medical care work. It is paid by the patient's medical insurance company. The Home Care Assistance Co. controls caretakers for the patient, who cook meals and feed the patient, give medications on schedules provided, keep the patients clean, and help them with natural needs. Insurance companies pay for the professional nursing work (e.g., Hospice Family Care Co.), but not for the work of Home Care Assistance-type work. Our costs for the services of the latter company (24/7) is about $3200/week. Marilyn was then under the care of the two service companies and staying at home. She is bed-ridden, and must be helped to do practically everything. I think that this system is OK except for the requirement that patients under Hospice Family Care-type care are not allowed to be saved if they go into a crisis. They are supposed to die comfortably. Thus, I never signed their requirement to order such a behavior, yet they still accepted Marilyn to benefit their services. And Marilyn has gone through two such events, where I refused her to stay home and die, rather than go to the hospital and be saved if at all possible.

And so, Marilyn was staying at home now, being taken care of by a nursing company whose goal is not to help the patient die comfortably, but to maintain the patient alive and attempt to develop normalcy if at all possible. She no longer had a catheter installed in the bladder, and was thus not constantly developing bladder infections like she used to suffer. Her colon has been removed and the small intestine now is terminated in an opening at the bottom of belly. The feces thus enter into an attached bag, which has to be emptied once a day. She felt much better than before. Thank God for that, and we hope that this situation will continue.

This second stay in the hospital by Marilyn took place in March, 2020 in the middle of the COVID-19 epidemic time. I was not allowed to see Marilyn in the hospital even once while she was there. I suppose that this was the correct action by the hospital administration, but it was really difficult not to see one's wife before surgery, which was predictably successful to only the extent of 40%. I am terribly thankful to the lord and the Chandler Hospital doctors who did such a successful surgical job, and that happy feeling overcomes tenfold my sadness for an inability to see my wife before such a dangerous operation. I hope the Lord will grant her many years.

But if one looks beyond my personal happy ending, the general degree of happiness and order in the U.S. population was not great. In fact, the order was a mess in the major U.S. cities. It started with an event in Minneapolis, Minnesota, where its police, in the end of May, 2020, had arrested a black individual by the name of George Floyd, who was supposedly trying to pass a counterfeit $20 bill. Mr. Floyd was handcuffed, and was being held down on the sidewalk with a knee on his neck by a policeman. The prisoner could not breathe and passed away. Well, the news immediately spread out all over the country with demands to abolish police in the U.S. and other similar nonsense. The Minneapolis policemen were fired and were tried for murder, but that wasn't enough: it became a "Federal case" with disorders in practically all large U.S. cities. Normally, the disorders last for a day or two, but this time, they have been lasting for more than a month and there doesn't seem to be an end to them. In fact, they seem to have been organized and well led. And another event to maintain the fire occurred in Atlanta, Georgia, where a policeman shot to death an inebriated black driver who tried to run away from the police after being stopped on the road. Was that necessary? The chief of police in Atlanta resigned thereupon. And in Seattle, the police were no longer able to control the "protests" going on, and in a marching order abandoned at least one of its neighborhoods.

With all this mayhem going on in the U.S., I was watching on my computer screen an event in Russia, quite opposite to those in the United States: the consecration of a brand new huge Orthodox church in Moscow that was termed as the main cathedral of the Russian armed forces. A copy of this event was sent to us by Father Alexander Cutler, a former priest of the Holy Trinity Orthodox Cathedral in Chicago where Marilyn and I were members when we lived there. Father Alexander had retired and moved to live in a Ukraine Orthodox monastery. He regularly sent us e-mails about the happenings of Ukrainian and Russian Orthodox churches; many thanks to him for sending us a film on that event. Patriarch Kirill, the head of the Russian Orthodox Church, was serving to consecrate the new church with a number of Orthodox bishops, priests, and deacons in the presence of numerous men in military uniforms and civilian folks. There was quite a difference between that event and the goings on Seattle streets where the police had abandoned it. This doesn't happen to me very often, but on that day, I wanted more to be present in Moscow rather than in Seattle.

And to mention another event that happened to me at approximately the same time as my viewing of the consecration procedure of the Moscow church was my discovery of a criminal happening that occurred to me for the first time in my life: someone had used my Shell credit card number to "buy" some $700-worth of Diesel fuel in a local gas station. This was done within a week or so; they tried to buy more, but they had already exceeded the maximum allowed on the card. I did not lose my Shell credit card, nor had I loaned it to anyone. How the thief learned my credit card number and my name I don't know; I am told that it is possible to place some kind of photo apparatus on the gas pump and copy the card when it gets inserted into the slot when gas is being bought. I had Marilyn's assistant call the Shell Company, and within a week I got a new card and a new bill for $31.19 instead of 711.19$. I immediately sent them the money. Though I got a new credit card, I never used it; my son Alex suggested that I drop it and pay cash for gas. I thought that it was the right suggestion, and since then I never had a problem when I used cash for gas, which I fill my tank with every week.

Marilyn Grib graduation from College
With a BA degree in Education

Anatoly Bezkorovainy

Holy Trinity RUSSIAN ORTHODOX CATHEDRAL

1121 No. Leavitt St. — CHICAGO 22, ILL.

Home of Anatoly and Mariyln In Lincolnwood, Illinois

Archbishop John marries Anatoly and Marilyn
at The Holy Trinity Cathedral

Newly wedded Marilyn with parents Nicholas and Paula Grib

Archbishop John at the Bezkorovainy
Marriage feast on June 8, 1964

Marriage license of Anatoly and Marilyn

Marilyn Bezkorovainy, the bride,
Dancing with her new father-in-law Ignaty Bezkorovainy

Marilyn Bezkorovainy and I did not want to return to the Soviet Union or countries occupied by the Soviet Union after World War II. This includes this book's author. These folks organized ROCOR parishes all over the U.S. A., and even moved their headquarters (Metropolitan's seat) from Serbia to New York (as the Communists took over Serbia/Yugoslavia after World War II). When the Soviet regime collapsed in Russia, the ROCOR church returned to the Russian Orthodox spiritual leadership in Moscow by acquiring an exarchate-type status. Chicago Bishop Peter Lukianov even informed me at a conversation that I was having with him that he had been one of several candidates to be elected the Patriarch of Russia, but someone else was elected instead of him (Archbishop Cyril). Bishop Peter was not terribly upset; maybe next time, he said with a laugh. The OCA remained independent/autocephalous.

I will now return to my story of getting married to Marilyn Grib. It was quite an event for us, a happy event. There were over 200 people, mostly Russians invited by our and Grib families, mostly from the Holy Trinity and Holy Virgin Protection churches, but there were plenty of other visitors. Bishop John of Riga and Chicago, who married us, was the guest of honor (fig. 2-2), and my brother George and Marilyn's cousin Barbara Saulnier were the man and the maid of honor. Fig 2-3 shows Marilyn's parents Nicholas and Paula Grib with Marilyn, fig. 2-4 shows my father dancing with Marilyn, and 2-5 shows the two of us alone. The 2-6 picture shows the marriage procedure with crowns over our heads.

After the festivities, the two of us drove to a nearby hotel where we had rented a room, and stayed there until about noon the next day. We left Chicago there and drove in Marilyn's Buick (I did not trust my Plymouth) to Terre Haute, Indiana where we stayed overnight. Our "honeymoon" lasted about a month: we drove all over the place in Florida, then went to visit Ames, Iowa for the last time in our lives, where we visited the cat that I had sprayed with cold water to stop his fight with another cat. And he still growled at me! And from Ammes, we headed home to our new apartment at 7730 North Ridge Ave., our new living quarters for our next 2-3 years, where Gregory, named after his grandfather, was born in May of the 1965th year. Marilyn and her mother, without my agreement, decided that she and her baby will stay with her mother, and I wasn't sure if she would eventually come back to our home and me. I could not figure out this whole thing, but lo and behold, she did come back to our home after some 8 weeks. The boy was baptized at the Holy Virgin Protection Church. The winter of 1967 was very snowy and there was a stretch of time when I could not get to work because nothing with wheels was moving in Chicago. Most of the time Greg feared going outside. But that was the last year that Marilyn, I, and Greg lived in a rental apartment. In 1968, Marilyn's Uncle John (Zickovich) told us that he had found a house for us that he thought we would like. We already had saved enough money for a house down-payment, and we were ready to move from our one-bedroom apartment to something bigger and Uncle John's find looked promising. The house was located in Lincolnwood, a near suburb of Chicago, on the corner of Pratt Ave. and Kilpatrick Street, one block East of Cicero Ave, and one block from the Edens Expressway, which could take you directly to downtown Chicago. The house had a one-car garage, since it was built around 1930 when 2-car families were not existent. It had 3 bedrooms on the second floor, 11/2 baths, and on the first floor, kitchen, dining and living rooms. Down below, was a full unfinished basement, very good for storage. The walls were made of lannon-stone. The price was $35,000, and we bought it. We stayed there for 20 years, until both kids were in college and we did not

CHAPTER 3

FORTY FOUR YEARS OF TEACHING AND RESEARCH ACTIVITIES

INTRODUCTION

This chapter is devoted to my work in the research laboratories either by myself or as a director of graduate students, technicians, and research associates (Ph. D.- level workers). This type of activity of mine lasted for 44 years, from the time I became a graduate student at the University of Illinois in Chicago (1956) to the year of my semi-retirement from the Rush Medical College in the year of 2000, when I went on a part-time status and stopped working in the laboratory. From 2000 to 2005 I worked at Rush Medical College and College of Podiatric Medicine teaching biochemistry to medical students. In 2005 (I was 70 years old), I quit working, and with my wife Marilyn moved from Lincolnwood (a Chicago suburb) to a provincial city in Northern Illinois by the name of Galena to enjoy its history and its countryside. We stayed there for 10 years, when, due to Marilyn's Parkinson's Disease, we moved to Sun Lakes, Arizona, a suburb of Chandler, which is a suburb of Phoenix, where our son Alex has been living for almost 20 years and teaching history at a Phoenix high school. In many ways, I now believe that it was a mistake, because in my opinion, the medical profession in Arizona is on a lower level as opposed to that of Illinois, even so in the village of Galena and especially in its nearby city (across the Mississippi River) of Dubuque, Iowa. But what has been done was done, and we have to live with our decisions.

GRADUATE SCHOOL

I started graduate school at the University of Illinois (its medical, dental, and pharmacy school complex on the Westside of Chicago's "Loop" area) in September of 1956, a month after I graduated with a BS degree in biochemistry from University of Chicago. My graduate school department in graduate school was also in the science of biochemistry, a basic science in medical school studies, whose chairman was Dr. Richard Winzler. For some reason he wanted me to work with him, and I did not complain. But being the chairman, he didn't have much time to spend with his graduate students, and thus, from the very beginning of my 4-year stay in his laboratory, I saw him very seldom, and my teacher had to be an older graduate student of his by the name of Tohru Inouye. Dr. Winzler had been at Illinois for only a couple of years before I arrived; he had come from the University of Southern California (as I recall) and Tohru Inouye was also from there and had been Dr. Winzler's student already there. So he became my real teacher! And it so happened that the two of us received our Ph. D. degrees in June, 1961, though I had already been working at the Oak Ridge National Laboratory for almost a year; all degrees at the Chicago University of Illinois were granted only once a year in June. Thus, I finished all my work in September, 1960, but had to wait until June of 1961 to officially get my diploma. It seems that Dr. Inouye was in no hurry to finish his studies, as I was. It took him 7-8 years to do so, and he was quite satisfied with that. He was of Japanese descent, born in California, and during World War II he served in the U. S. army as a Japanese language interpreter. After the war, he was married to a wonderful lady, also of the Nisei background, who was working at a Chicago downtown clothing store as a buyer of goods to be resold. Because of her job, and perhaps because of Tohru's inheritances, they were not poor (like most of our graduate students were), they lived on the 60th floor of Chicago's North Michigan Ave. building from where you could see Chicago's White Sox baseball games, and every other year, Tohru bought a new Buick automobile. So he was not in a hurry to finish his work for his Ph. D. degree; life was good, and his professor, Dr. Winzler, was not pushing him. Tohru got a job at Chicago's Children's Memorial Hospital after graduation, and as I recall, one of his accomplishments was to write and publish a multi-volume book on children's diseases. I have been most grateful to him for his help with teaching me how to handle procedures to do my research projects, e.g., how to work with ion exchange chromatography while our boss was in Washington giving his opinions on American universities' research grant applications to the National Institutes of Health research grant money sources.

While I was a graduate student, I learned the laboratory work on protein chemistry, much with the help of Tohru Inouye, my colleague and friend. Among such procedures were the electrophoresis methods, chromatography techniques, colorimetric methods, etc. So my first dissertation that I wrote was for a Masters degree, which I got in the year of 1958. In my dissertation project, I attempted to isolate the thyroxine-binding protein from human plasma, but the attempt was not successful. I could identify the protein by adding the radioactive thyroxine to human plasma, whereby, upon electrophoresis the radioactive material was moving with albumin and an alpha-two protein at pH 8.6, suggesting that the specific thyroxine-binding protein was an alpha two-globulin, which at pH 4.5 moved with the M-2 proteins, but I was not successful in isolating it. But my attempt did show that there was a thyroxine binding protein in human serum, which belonged to the alpha-2/M-2 group of proteins, most likely a glycoprotein among several others of this type. I was awarded the MS-degree for my work, but my professor did not think that it was good enough to publish.

My dissertation for the Ph. D. degree was concerned with the isolation of a glycoprotein that was also an M-2 electrophoretically, but it did not bind thyroxine. It was isolated in a pure state, and I did a number of determinations on it. It was isolated by a carboxymethylcellulose column, which also delivered pure orosomucoid, previously isolated by Schmid and by Winzler, who was at that time in California. My method was, however, much easier for its isolation as opposed to Schmid's or Winzler's. Like the thyroxine-binding protein of my MS-degree, it was a glycoprotein, it did not show an N-terminal amino acid, its sedimentation constant was 2.35 s compared to 2.60 s for orosomucoid, and its carbohydrate content was 20% compared to 40% for orosomucoid. Its entire amino acid content was not reported, but the amounts of tryptophan and tyrosine were 4.2% and 1.7%, while those for the M-2 protein were 6.5% and 6.1% for the new M-2, respectively. But as indicated above, it did not bind thyroxine. The paper describing the new M-2 protein was published by A. Bezkorovainy and R. Winzler in Biochimica & Biophysica Acta 49:559-565, 1961.

POST-DOCTORAL POSITIONS IN OAK RIDGE, TENNESSEE AND AMES, IOWA

After I left Chicago in September, 1960, I continued to work on acid glycoproteins along with other problems that were of interest to my bosses: first at Oak Ridge National Laboratory, and a year later, at National Animal Disease Laboratory in Ames, Iowa. Thus, for the next two years, I basically tried to finish my job on the nature of the M-2 proteins of mammalian plasmas, that in addition to the jobs that my employers wished me to do. I had to work with bovine blood, since both in Oak Ridge and Ames there was no way to get human plasma. And even in Chicago, I had to use Cohn's Fraction VI of human plasma, which had the proteins that I was interested in. This plasma fraction VI was commercially available at companies that were selling biological materials, and it had gone through several chemical physical procedures that could have altered the proteins that I was interested in. In Oak Ridge and Ames, I had no access to human blood, but I could have bovine blood in quantities: in Oak Ridge, I had the packing house workers bleed the animals after they had killed them by shooting with a gun; I took the blood to the lab and immediately centrifuged it to get the plasma and platelets. I used the platelets for another project in which my boss at Oak Ridge, Dr. Dave Doherty, was interested in. And plasma I used to isolate the M-1 and M-2 proteins by an ammonium sulfate precipitation procedure that I had developed to obtain bovine orosomucoid and other acid proteins. My boss Dr. Dave Doherty and I published an article comparing human and bovine orosomucoide (Nature 195:1003, 1962).

In Oak Ridge I isolated an M-2 glycoprotein from Jersey bovine animal plasma (Bezkorovainy and Doherty, Archives of Biochemistry and Biophysics, 96:491, 1962), and thoroughly characterized it. It was isolated by my ammonium sulfate/carboxymethyl cellulose column procedure. It binds thyroxine very vigorously (Bezkorovainy and Doherty, Biochim. Biophys. Acta 58:124, 1962). When I moved to Ames, Iowa and used plasma of a Holstein animal, which had not been slaughtered, but was "medically" bled, to use as a source of the M-2 protein, which in Oak Ridge bound thyroxine, after using the identical procedure to isolate it, and finding identical properties including amino acid contents, I found exactly zero, nil... ability to bind thyroxine (Bezkorovainy, Biochemistry 2:10, 1963). Why there was a difference between the plasmas of Tennessee and Iowa animals, I could not figure out. But some 10 years later, I read an article by someone else who "discovered" a thyroxine-binding property of bovine plasma; I just don't remember who it was. But to return to the Tennessee bovine blood platelets, I tried to gather a supply from the Tennessee animals, but could not get enough of them free of white and red blood cells, and thus dropped that project at that time. A couple of years later, however, when I was back in Chicago and working in the Rush-Presbyterian-St. Luke's Hospital, I was telling the platelet story to my boss, Dr. Max Rafelson (Biochemistry Department chair), and he got interested, by George, and "forced" me to develop a study of these cells. I even got a technician to get it started; yet I wasn't particularly interested in that area, but if your boss wants to do it, how can you say no? Platelets are, of course, blood cells that participate in the coagulation of blood. I was able to get enough of human blood to isolate platelets (they were much easier to clean up than the bovine ones were), and I was able to do a bit of original work on them. I found that some 15% of platelet content was fibrinogen; no wonder that platelets favor blood clotting. There was also some 2% of serum albumin, but no other blood proteins. There was a considerable amount of glycogen in combination of the glycogen binding protein, as well as lactate dehydrogenase of the heart type. We published a paper on that work (Bezkorovainy and Rafelson, J. Lab. Clinical Med. 64:212, 1964). My boss, Dr. Max Rafelson, wrote a grant application to the NIH asking for money to study platelets further; I recall that he included me in that as well, and he was successful. He had funds for this work for some 4 years, as I recall. But I wasn't too eager to participate, and got my own grants to do other things. Dr. Rafelson then hired a helper to do the job; his name was Dr. Booyse, he was of South African nationality and quite eager to succeed. As I recall, they had some success in their work, but no Nobel prizes were awarded. But let me return to the early 1960's, to Oak Ridge and Ames, Iowa.

I stayed in Oak Ridge, Tennessee for one year (1960 to 1961). I had rented a studio apartment to live in for $55/month. It was the first time that I lived alone and on my own, without any relatives nearby. I was 25 years old, and had to get used to some daily duties, which were previously done by my mother. One such item was cooking dinners; when I arrived, I went to the store, got some food items, and cooked a soup for my first dinner in my own apartment. On the next day I woke up with a terrible pain in the belly, which did not get restrained for a week. I had to miss one week of work, which I had never done before. Since then, I never cooked any lunches or dinners for myself; other than making a sandwich and a cup of tea or coffee, I cooked no food for myself and had all meals at a restaurant. And there was one across the street from my apartment building, where I ate every day, sometimes with a friend from Norway, a Dr. Froholm, who was also a post-doc at the Oak Ridge Laboratory. I stayed there for a year, even though they wanted me to remain there as a permanent employee. Pretty much all the professional folks in my Biology Division were from Northern America; like my boss, Dr. Dave Doherty, was born in New York, and received his doctorate in biochemistry at the University of Wisconsin. My fellow post-doc in Dr. Doherty's lab was from northern New York State with a Ph. D. from the University of Illinois at Champaign-Urbana. But all the lower-level employees were locals, the Southerners, like the female technician who was appointed to help me by the big boss (Dr. Alexander Hollander). I took her on dates a couple of times, but the connection did not occur: too many cultural differences. But Dr. Hollander was an interesting fellow. He spoke with a heavy German accent, and his expertise was using radioactive materials in the field of biological sciences; more precisely, the effects: of radiation on human biology. Every Sunday he used to take a bunch of post-docs (like me) and permanent worker scientists to explore the country sides of Tennessee. I remember best visiting inactive surface coal mining areas, with abandoned villages where the miners used to live. What was most interesting there were fossils of plants spread all over the place. I collected a bunch of them: petrified tree branches, copies of leaves impressed in flat rocks, petrified plant roots, etc. Dr. Hollander had a collection of these, exhibited in his office, including a petrified trunk of a fairly thick tree. He liked me, and perhaps that's why I was offered a permanent job there; and he liked me because I was translating for him scientific papers from Russia, which were of interest to him. There was apparently no one around Oak Ridge who could translate scientific literature from Russian into English. Pretty pathetic, I think!

Well, while I was working in Oak Ridge, the U.S. Department of Agriculture attempted to staff its newly built research laboratory assembly in the outskirts of Ames, Iowa. The reason why Ames, Iowa was chosen for the lab's location was because Iowa State University was there; it contained one of the best agricultural colleges in the United States. And they were employing basic scientists along with veterinarians. They offered me a job at a newly organized biochemistry department, whose leader was a former professor of Minnesota State University (Dr. Roepke); he knew Dr. Winzler, who recommended me for a job as a new USDA GS-12 chemist. I was glad to accept, because Ames is "only" 310 miles from Chicago and I could easily drive to spend a weekend there to see Marilyn and my parents, and the pay was some 20% higher than that in Oak Ridge. The distance of Oak Ridge from Chicago was some 600 miles (there were not too many 4-lane highways in the U.S. yet), and around Louisville, Kentucky, the bridge across the Mississippi River had only one lane in each direction. So it took hours to get through that city into Indiana, and after I managed to do that, I was always so tired that I had to stay the night in the nearest motel on the road. And so, after spending a year at Oak Ridge, I moved "lock, stock, and barrel" to Ames Iowa. Before getting there, I had rented a small apartment, a la Oak Ridge, near the Iowa State University, a short drive from the National Animal Disease Laboratory, my working place. On the first night, I was inundated by cockroaches, and in the morning, I moved to a local hotel where I stayed for about a week until I found a room for rent ($40/month). It was located in a private house owned by an Iowa State engineer, who had rented another bedroom to an Iowa State University student. The owner slept in the house's third bedroom and he was single. I had a separate bathroom attached to my room, my fellow renter was a quiet chap, and the owner was usually pretty quiet as well, except that once in a while he organized parties, to which I was invited, that lasted almost all Saturday night. He also had a cat, which he let out every evening for the night, and let it back home in the morning. Every once in a while, the cat had a fight with some competitor, sometimes close to my window, so I could hear all that when I was trying to sleep. I usually broke up the battle by throwing a bucket of water on the competitors. After my wife and I were married (1964), we stopped in Ames on our honeymoon trip to Florida; I asked the cat owner where the animal was, and he said he was sleeping in the garage. I went there to say hello, but when the cat woke up, he growled at me threateningly; he did not remember me, and I left him alone.

BACK TO CHICAGO

After I moved to the Rush Presbyterian St. Luke's Medical Center in 1962 (I was also appointed non salaried Assistant Professor at the University of Illinois Medical College). My research activities were still connected with plasma glycoproteins, the M-2's, orosomucoid, thyroxine-binding protein, and such. In order to avoid using commercial plasma alcohol fractionation compositions, I developed my own plasma fractionation procedure using ammonium sulfate and changes of pH in order to obtain the M-2 plasma fractions that were supposed to bind thyroxine. Thus, 300 g of ammonium sulfate were added to 1 liter of plasma at O degrees C., and pH was adjusted to 4.6 with HCI. The precipitate was removed and pH adjusted to 3.7. The precipitate, amounting to about 1000 mg, was isolated, and the supernatant was used to isolate glycoproteins M-1 and M-2. The precipitate consisted of 50-60% of a protein called transferrin, which was an iron-binding protein. It was further purified by chromatography on a DEAE cellulose column, which yielded 350 mg of transferrin per liter of plasma (A. Bezkorovainy, M. Rafelson, and V. Likhite, Archives Biochem. Biophys.103:371, 1963). The transferrin developed from human plasma by this procedure, and later, when it became commercially available, was the basis for my research efforts for the next 10 to 15 years.

Several graduate students and post-doctoral fellows in our laboratory used this procedure and eventually the commercially-available transferrin to study its method of binding iron, its structure, and its biological function. One outstanding graduate student was Rainer H. Zschocke from Germany. He was married and had a child with his wife when he joined my lab as a graduate student around 1970. He was working in my lab for some 4 years until he received the Ph. D. degree and went back to Germany with his family to take a job as head of research in a pharmaceutical company. He was very successful there with his work, but unexpectedly, while he was out of his home town on business, he committed suicide by shooting himself. In Germany, very few persons are given permission to own firearms, not like it is in the U. S., so it was somewhat unbelievable to me that this was what happened. But this is what his wife wrote to me later. God bless his soul! While he was with us, he did enough work to write some 5 research papers with me on protein chemistry, plus two review articles in the German journal "Arzneimittel-

Forschung" entitled "Structure and Function of Transferrin Parts I and II," (vol. 24, pp. 476- 485 and 726-737, 1974). I think that his name on two articles in a German journal helped him to get his important job in a German pharmaceutical company. His demise stopped the progression of a research scientist with a great future. The other articles recording his work in my laboratory were as follows: Journal of Immunology 104:648,1970; Biochimica et Biophysica Acta 181:295, 1969 and 200;60, 1970; European J. Biochem. 27:145,1972. The authors of them were Zschocke and Bezkorovainy.

Towards the end of the 1960's our work on transferrin was going in full speed ahead, but all of a sudden a paper appears in a Swedish journal that says that transferrin is a protein with two polypeptide chains with one iron-binding site on each chain and with a molecular weight of 40,000 each (J. O. Jeppsson. Acta chem. Scand. 21:1686, 1967). We attempted to duplicate their results, but could not. We believed that the Swedish ultracentrifuge didn't work right, and showed the sedimentation constant to be half of what others did, including ours. Our results were published in Biochemical Journal, vol. 110, p. 765, year of 1968. The molecular weight of transferrin remains at about 80,000 with a single polypeptide chain, whose rope model remains. No one has yet confirmed Jeppsson's results.

Thus, the work that was being done in the late 1960's at my Rush laboratory was largely concerned with serum transferrin and its physiology. A summary of some achievements we published in Rush's Medical Bulletin (vol. 9, No. 1, January, 1970,pp. 6-14). The work was continued in the 1970's by some graduate students and post-doctoral fellows. The main worker was my technician, Dietmar Grohlich (a German immigrant), who has been my co-author on a number of publications, e. g., Biochimica et Biophysica Acta 310:365, 1973; 147:497, 1967; 214:37, 1970; and 263:645, 1972. He was attending classes at the University of Illinois while he was working with me; he received his BS degree, and then entered the University of Illinois Graduate College, Department of Pathology, into their Ph. D. program. I was an unpaid faculty member of that University department along with the Biochemistry Department, and was thus able to accept Dietmar as my Ph. D. student. And so after a few years, he graduated from the University of Illinois with a Ph. D. degree in Pathology, and in 1979, he was hired by the State of Illinois police to run their narcotics laboratory. He stayed there for 20 years and retired at the same time as I did from Rush. He and his wife moved to

Florida because its weather was best for her health. They had a daughter, born in Chicago, whose godfather was I. She became a nurse, got married, and is still working at a Chicago suburban hospital. Dietmar's wife, unfortunately, passed away in the 2010's. He was and is a good friend of mine and was an excellent assistant when he was working with me. God grant him many years!

Another student of mine who did some classic work on the transferrin class of proteins was William Line, now of blessed memory. He determined the amino acid side-chains that bind iron to transferrin: 2 histidine and 3 tyrosine side-chains, plus a bicarbonate molecule per iron atom (Biochemistry 6:3393, 1967). He also worked on the structure of lactoferrin, a transferrin-like protein present in bovine, as well as human milk, which binds iron just like transferrin does (Internatl. J. Biochemistry 7:203, 1976). After he finished his doctorate work with me, he went to work for the Miller Brewing Company of Milwaukee, Wisconsin, 'where he was one of the inventors of light beers. He was married to our good friend Dr. Michele Melyn, a pediatric neurologist, who remained in the Chicago area after he moved to Wisconsin. He passed away after his retirement around 2010 A. D.

I think that the 1960's and 1970's were my most productive research years. I felt that the next part of work on transferrin had to be amino acid sequence determination, a very tedious and difficult process with much equipment that I didn't have, nor did I have any experience in the process of amino acid sequencing of protein structures. Normally, if one wants to do research in an area that one hadn't had experience with, one usually goes on a "sabbatical" leave for 6 months in another laboratory where such experts are, and then comes back to one's own laboratory with a new expertise, let's say, of amino acid sequence determination in proteins. I got started on my own with that kind of an effort when, with Dr. Grohlich's help, we were able to split transferrin into several pieces with cyanogens bromide (proteins are split by CNBr at their methionine residues; there are 7-8 methionine residues in transferrin), to isolate them, and determine their amino acid and carbohydrate content, their molecular weights, and Nterminal groups. We had a total of 6 transferrin fragments with molecular weights of 26,000, 16,000, 15,000, 9000, 6000, and 4000, for a total of 76,000, close enough for the time being to the 80,000 molecular weights of intact transferrin (Bezkorovainy and Grohlich, Biochim. Biophys. Acta 310:365, 1973). We did not proceed any further, nor did I take a sabbatical leave to learn how to determine amino acid sequences of proteins. I stayed at home as my kids were growing up and my wife needed my assistance to take care of the boys. But someone else (I forget the name) eventually determined the amino acid sequence of transferrin and went on from there. And I was getting busier with the medical school and establishment of a graduate college at Rush, plus arrival of new post-doctoral fellows who had their own ideas on what they wanted to do. And all this forced me and my lab to change directions and drop attempts to determine amino acid sequences of transferrin and other proteins.

In those early years of my life at Rush Medical College, in the 1960's and 1970's, I had a few other graduate students and even post-docs. The students, like Drs. Zschocke, Line, and Grohlich were graduates (Ph. D.) students of the University of Ulinois, who did their dissertation research in my, a University of Illinois professor's, laboratory. In addition to these three, I had a few other students who did their dissertation work with me, though these were less noticeable than the others mentioned above. One of them, Claire Gerbeck, was really Dr. Rafelson's (our chairman's) student, but like Dr. Winzler and I, Dr. Rafelson and Ms. Gerbeck couldn't meet that much, and I was Ms. Gerbeck's Tohru Inouye. Her thesis concerned haptoglobins, hemoglobin-binding proteins of serum, and she had a couple of nice papers published with Dr. Rafelson and me as co-authors ("Studies on a glycopeptide obtained from human haptoglobin," Biochim. Biophys. Acta 101:229, 1965; and "Glycopeptide obtained from human haptoglobin 2-1 and 2-2," Biochemistry 6:403, 1965). And there also was my student, Dr. Marie T. Chiao, who studied hemoglobin-haptoglobin interaction, who also published two papers based on her dissertation: Biochim. Biophys. Acta 263:60, 1972, and Physical Chemistry and Physics 3:394, 1971. Dr. Chiao, as far as I heard, had entered a medical school after earning her Ph. D. degree, and beyond that, I haven't heard anything about her. By the way, haptoglobins are serum glycoproteins that bind hemoglobin and proceed to have it metabolized. The individuals I described above were my graduate students in the 1960's and 1970's. They were basically University of Illinois students who did their research work with me in my laboratory at the Rush Medical College. They were all very successful individuals and I am very proud of them. In the 1980's, however, my employer, the Rush University, started its own graduate school, and I was involved in the same way in their teaching. But they had no connection with the University of Illinois. Before getting into that group, I would like to mention another, much smaller group of "students," the post-doctoral fellows, which were not connected to the University of Illinois or Rush University. They were simply temporary employees of Rush-Presbyterian-St. Luke's Medical Center.

My first post-doctoral fellow was Dr. Dayle Sly; I do not remember where she got her Ph. D. degree, but she came to Rush to get post-doctoral experience and spent a few years in my lab. She took part in several projects of mine, as a principal investigator in some and co-investigator in others. For instance, she determined that the C-terminal amino acid of transferrin was proline, which for some reason was difficult to determine (Physiological Chemistry and Physics 6:171, 1974), and how iron-saturated transferrin penetrates the reticulocyte cell wall to deliver iron thereto (Biochim. Biophys. Acta 385:36, 1975). She was co-author on 3 other publications from our laboratory; a very excellent scientist and worker. Dr. Sly stayed at Rush for some 3 years, and then went to work with Amoco Research Center in Naperville, Illinois. We also had an on and off (unpaid) worker, who started to visit our lab when she was a medical student at the University of Illinois: Robin Miller. She simply liked to work in the laboratory and became registered as the hospital "volunteer" or some such title. She worked in our lab as much as she could, and I sometimes included her name in published research papers. She graduated from the University of Illinois Medical School and then took residency in Pathology, I believe also at the University of Illinois Hospital. Eventually, she finished that duty and got a job that required writing some pathology texts, especially on the illness of polio, which happened soon after the Salk vaccine hit the market. All this time, she regularly came to our lab and worked on our experimental issues. She also married her pathology professor, Dr. Catchpole, either during her residency or after it, who was some 30 years older than she was. They purchased a 1870's townhouse almost in the downtown of Chicago, and spent their free time getting it repaired and modernized. Eventually, she decided that she wanted to get a Ph. D. degree in biochemistry as well, and was accepted in our graduate college (after we had organized the Rush Graduate College in the 1980's). She started her research project with me, but became sick with breast cancer and passed away at the age of 50. We published the work that she had completed for her thesis, and upon our department's request, the Rush Medical College granted her a post mortem Ph.D. degree. Rest in peace, Robin Miller-Catchpole, M. D., Ph.D.!

In the early 1970's, I got a call from a colleague of mine, Dr. Georg Springer from Evanston Hospital/Northwestern University in regard to a postdoctoral fellow, Dr. Jim Nichols, from his laboratory, who was looking for a job, and he, Dr. Springer, did not have enough money to keep him even though he wanted to. Dr. Springer was a member of the German family owners of Springer Verlag, a German medical publishing house. He was basically a biochemist working on blood group substances and such, and we were collaborating on some projects of common interests now and then. Well, Dr. Jim Nichols was a Ph. D. graduate of Northwestern University, one of the best universities in the state of Illinois, and he had trouble getting a job so he had applied for a post office job to be able to support his family. Was this so because he was an African-American? I had some extra money in my grants, and I grabbed him. And Dr. Springer and I were not mistaken; he turned out to be an excellent scientist and worker, and chances are that he could have easily gotten a job as an Assistant Professor in a college after leaving my laboratory, say in 3 years or so. But something else happened after his working in my laboratory for 3 years: he entered the Rush Medical College and became a physician instead of a college professor, sometime in the late 1970's. He was practicing medicine until the second decade of the year 2000, if I am not mistaken, when I got a call from the Chicago State University asking me to send reprints of his publications that we wrote when he was my post-doctoral fellow; he had applied there for a professorship. It seems that he had retired from being a doctor and had applied to return to his old profession-(bio)chemistry professorship. I hope he had gotten the job. But I have not yet mentioned Dr. Nichols' successful years in our Rush laboratory. As I expected, we were able to publish some great papers from his work, for instance, "Glycoproteins from Mature Human Milk Whey," Pediatric Research 10:1, 1976; "Isolation of Several Glycoproteins from Human Colostrum Whey, " Biochim. Biophys. Acta 412:99, 1975; "Glycoproteins from Human Colostrum," Biochem. J. 135:875, 1973, and several others. Since I was the biochemistry course director in our medical school, I released him from taking biochemistry when he started medical school at Rush. He had thus some extra time (not that he needed it) to handle the other first-year courses such as anatomy, histology, physiology, psychology, etc. He graduated in the normal 4 years with few if any difficulties that other black students often had, and I assume that being a good biochemist he also became a good doctor, and a good example for all of us. May the Lord grant him many years

But getting back to Rush Medical College in the late 1970's, the Biochemistry's chairman, Dr. Max Rafelson had been appointed some kind of a dean, and a new chairman for the Biochemistry Department was appointed (I don't remember if there was a search committee involved). But the new chair turned out to be Dr. Howard Sky-Peck, who was a member of another hospital department (which one, I don't remember). He was an older gentleman, a veteran of World War II, but in the British forces rather than American ones (which was the situation with Dr. Rafelson). He was an expert on kidney biochemistry, and had superb experience with the clinical chemistries of kidney functions. During his tenure as Biochemistry chair, Rush was separating from its connections with University of Illinois, and as I recall, we the faculty were being released from our faculty connections with Illinois. We thus were losing our unpaid professorships from the University of Illinois and no longer could have Illinois graduate students who were in the past doing research for their M.S. and Ph. D. degrees with us. And thus, the Rush University established its own graduate college from our "basic science" departments such as biochemistry, psychology, and pathology. But the other basic science departments are capable of granting Ph. D. degrees had to be organized. We already had Rush professors to teach medical students who did not belong to any anatomy, physiology, pharmacology, etc. departments because such did not exist, but these professors were members of medical/surgical departments, and their specific departments had to be established in order to be able to begin granting Ph. D. degrees in those subjects. And such new departments had to be approved by the state of Illinois, as the already extant departments (e.g., biochemistry) had to be approved by the state as well. And we were the first department to request the State of Illinois to give us permission to grant students M. S. and Ph. D. degrees in biochemistry. After all, we were basically doing it already for the University of Illinois, and we were sure that the state would give us the appropriate permission without any difficulty. The "permissions" committee that the state appointed for us consisted entirely of Illinois' Medical College Biochemistry Department's professors, our colleagues in the past, and our friends, or so we thought. One of them was especially hostile towards me because... I had a law degree. They were also terribly unhappy about Dr. Sky-Peck... I could not figure it out: their department had granted a good number of graduate students their Ph. D. degrees for their dissertations that they did under my and my colleagues' direction (e.g., Dr. Rafelson and Dr. Hayashi) and nobody complained about it then; now, my law degree made that somehow different... Well, how do I know what the real reason was for their flunking us? But who was blamed for all this by our administration? It was Dr. Sky-Peck, our chairman. He got sick, resigned his chairmanship, and a new search committee was organized. I was appointed a member thereof. I was a bit naive about such; I thought that we would be looking for the best candidate from the whole country of the U. S. I suggested a Professor Philip Aisen from New York whom I knew reasonably well because of our common interests in transferrin and iron metabolism. He was a super scientist, with both an M. D. and Ph.D. degrees. We had him invited for an interview, and it seemed that he liked our organization and the committee liked him. But all of a sudden we received from our committee's chair the CV of a scientist from our own Orthopedics Department, a biochemist by the name of Dr. Klaus Kuettner, whom the chairman of our committee announced to be a strong candidate. I knew him reasonably well, he was a good scientist, but nobody knew before that he was interested in the job. If I had known that he was interested, I would have been glad to vote for him in the first place and would not have bothered Dr. Aisen to take a trip to Chicago. Dr. Kuettner was thus elected chair of the Biochemistry Department.

THE DR. KLAUS KUETTNER ERA

D r. Klaus Kuettner was a Ph. D. scientist whose research interests were biochemistry of bones and other connective tissues, and that is why he was a member of Rush's Orthopedics Department. He was a great grant getter, which is always a property being looked for by search committees. I was wondering if he was offered a chairmanship by some other university, and our organization then offered him our Biochemistry Department chairmanship so they would not lose a super grant getter like Klaus. I never found out. And he really enlarged our department, brought in numerous grants, and hired a large number of young faculty members, largely to do research, and increased our number of graduate students to some 20 from perhaps 5 or so that we had at one time. Klaus was a German immigrant, with his Ph. D. received in Switzerland. After he became the chairman, he immediately organized another attempt to receive state approval for M. S. and Ph. D. granting (he told the state not to send any University of Illinois judges), and our rights to grant those graduate degrees was approved by the state without any further efforts. He had me promoted to a full professor, and made me Associate Chairman of the Biochemistry Department in charge of all educational activities, including teaching biochemistry to medical students, graduate students, medical technology and nursing students. Since we now had our own graduate program, we had to develop graduate level biochemistry courses, which our students would have to take after passing biochemistry taken by medical students. I taught medical student biochemistry (with Dr. Colin Morley, see below) and also portions of advanced graduate student courses. I also taught a course listed as Science and the Law, where I handled legal aspects of various topics such as patent laws, food and drug regulations, contracts etc; this after I passed my bar exam in 1977. I was also in charge of our department's Ph.D. program. Klaus was able to get some financing for our graduate program, which paid graduate students stipends of $10,000/year. We were supposed to accept 4 graduate students a year. We, of course, had a much larger number of applicants, especially from China, who were mostly M. D.'s. Unofficially, we tried to accept 2 Chinese (or other foreign) students a year, plus 2 Americans. But even that didn't work too well: the Chinese students (many but not all) would start the schooling, but after a year they would apply for immigrant status, and when they would get that, they would quit graduate school, get an internship in a hospital and do all the other things to acquire rights to practice medicine in the U.S. And most of them were pretty smart and well trained in medicine, and were thus successful. Yet some of them were honest, and continued their Ph. D. training to the end. One such student, Dr. Xianwen Vi, chose to work with me, and received his Ph. D. and is now working as biochemist in the University of North Carolina after taking a postdoctoral stint at the University of Illinois in Champaign-Urbana. Thus, it was difficult to predict which Chinese doctor would maintain his presence as a graduate student after arrival in the U.S., and which wanted to come to the U.S. with an intention to simply immigrate and then enter the American medical profession. Dr. Yi was an honest man; he had his name on two papers taken from his dissertation: Xianwen Yi, Eva Kot, and Anatoly Bezkorovainy, "Properties of NADH Oxidase from Lactobacillus delbrueckii ssp. bulgaricus," J. Sci. Food Agric. 78:527, 1998, and A. Bezkorovainy, Xianwen Yi, and Eva Kot, "Hydrogen peroxide production and ferric hydroxide binding by lactic acid bacteria," Recent Res. Devel. In Nutrition 1:49, 1996.

With Dr. Kuettner's arrival as Biochemistry Department's chairman and his successful effort to squeeze from the administration some $10,000 per year per student for "assistantships," we soon had some 10 graduate students in our department. And for so many students, we needed more professors, six of whom we soon hired upon Dr. Kuettner demanding or begging from Rush's administration. They were all young men and women Assistant Professors whose research interests were those of Dr. Klaus Kuettner: connective tissue metabolism and disorders. They also developed a graduate student course in this field, and thus, most new graduate students did their research with the young faculty. We usually had some 25 to 30 applicants for admission to our Ph. D. program, out of which, I (as the director of graduate program) selected 10 most successful candidates and presented them for selection by our admissions committee, of which I was the chair. They selected four to be admitted with two substitutes in case one or two of the four changed their minds.

With the arrival of Dr. Kuettner on the scene, my responsibilities at Rush increased by 2 to 3-fold compared to the past, and this made it almost impossible to write applications for grants. And to help me, my boss assigned for me a research assistant at the department's costs to help me with research.

The "lucky" candidate that was appointed was Eva Kot, M. S., who was a research assistant to a Neurology Department member that had left the institution. She remained with me until I retired from full-time work at Rush, at which time she too retired as she was about my age. Eva Kot was my co author on all the research papers that I published thenceforth. So we worked together very successfully, including Mrs. Kot's assistance to train my graduate students at doing the techniques that she used our research work. And so, the beginning of the 1980's was a change in my research activities. Slowly, the work on transferrin and iron metabolism was reduced and substituted by biochemistry of milk glycoproteins, bifidobacteria, and lactobacilli. Before the 1980's, I was interested most of the time on iron-binding proteins such as transferrins, yet I also kept attention on other topics, such as written in my review article in Journal of Dairy Science "Physical and Chemical Properties of Bovine Milk and Colostrum Whey M-1 Glycoproteins (J. Dairy Science 50:1368, 1967). Ten years later, I wrote another review article, this time on human milk proteins, "Human Milk and Colostrum Proteins: a Review," J. Dairy Science 60:1023, 1977. It was a review of several milk and colostrums proteins that had been isolated and characterized in the past few years to basically start on a much more serious attention to milk proteins and their biological activities, as well as the function of useful bacteria that help the development of human infants. I had a few graduate students during the 1980–2000-time frame, as well as Eva Kot, who did much of the research work that we published in the literature during that era: We had a couple of post-doctoral fellows, and a couple of undergraduate pre-medical students who eventually became physicians. As I recall, the students were Mark Poch, Nancy Topouzian, Xianwei Yi, and Robin Miller-Catchpole, who all ended up with Ph. D. degrees. In my entire career, I had only 10 graduate students who earned their Ph. D. degrees under my guidance, and I had some 6 post-doctoral fellows. All of them have been successful, and I hope that this was enough for a lifetime.

In the late 1970's, the administration hired a biochemist for our department to "help" us to teach the medical students; I don't know on whose advice, but the chairman at that time was Dr. Sky-Peck, and this perhaps was his idea. I was at that time the course director of biochemistry, and I had never complained about too much work or anything else. But Colin Morley, Ph. D. was hired as Assistant Professor and joined our staff. He was an Englishman, who went to Australia to get his Ph. D. degree, and after that he had some teaching experience there. He was indeed a good teacher and his British accent was much in his favor; my Slavic accent was OK, but it could not ever compete successfully with the British one (or even German, for that matter). Dr. Morley had no research plans, and was attached to my group of researchers to participate in my research interests. He published a number of manuscripts with my group, mostly on iron metabolism in hepatocytes, which cells were of Dr. Morley's expertise. It was successfully united with our expertise on iron metabolism. The basic issue that he was investigating was how iron (Fe^{++} or transferrin-bound Fe^{+++}) is taken up by isolated hepatocytes and what happens to iron after it enters such cells. Thus, instead of iron uptake by bacteria that my group was studying, his issue was how iron uptake takes place in the hepatocytes (liver cells). Some examples of Morley's publications were, for instance, "The behavior of transferrin receptors in rat hepatocyte plasma membranes," Clinical Physiol. Biochem. 1:318, 1983 by Morley and Bezkorovainy; "Iron metabolism pathways in the rat hepatocytes," Clin. Physiol. Biochem. 1,3,1983 by Morley, Rewers, and Bezkorovainy, and "The behavior of transferrin receptors on rat hepatocytes," in "Structure and function of iron storage and transport proteins" (Urushizaki et al., eds.), by Morley, delMastro, and Bezkorovainy "'

So, Dr. Morley's research was related to mine and his projects were carried out by the same technicians who were helping me. His research work was related basically to transferrin and its iron transport into the liver cells. Dr. Morley was or was not asking for grants (I don't know). He workedwith my technicians and we were writing common papers (I have 10 research papers that carry our two names as authors). I don't know if he received any grants to do research. He was eventually promoted to Associate Professor, and the dean made him an Assistant Dean, and thus he ceased to do research and work with me. Our last paper (with both our names) was published in 1985. Eventually, he was appointed to some other position in the administration, and then left Rush to work with a national organization that takes care of medical examinations. Some years later, I heard that he was a real estate salesman in the Indiana suburbs of Chicago, and then I heard that he came down with some cancer and passed away at the age of 60. After his demise, I couldn't stop thinking about Dr. Morley's possible career at Rush if he weren't so eager to get to the top of Rush administration. First of all, he wasn't an M. D., and in our institution that would've helped his career. An exception was my boss Dr. Klaus Kuettner. He was not an M. D. neither, but he managed to become chair of the Biochemistry Department. The reason was his ability to get grants and perhaps his German accent. Dr. Alexander Hollander, Oak Ridge Laboratory director when I was there, spoke with a heavy German accent; yet I was told that he spoke in perfect American English to his wife when no one else (especially from the Lab) was listening. In the scientific community, having a German background and/or accent has an advantage. And as far as Dr. Kuettner was concerned, I had never seen anyone as successful as he was even though he had never won the Nobel prize or was even close to that. The German accent was (and is?) helpful for getting ahead in science administration, a habit that started in the 19th century when science was practically a German monopoly. And an English accent, a la Dr. Morley, had a close second place to the German one. Except that it did not help Dr. Morley to become a department chairman. He tried to advance, perhaps toward a deanship? But it didn't work out. He was a good teacher and scientist, and he could have waited until I retired and he could then have had my job. But perhaps it was not enough and he wanted more. Rest in peace, Colin!

SCIENTIFIC LITERATURE: REVIEW ARTICLES

Review articles or papers are written for a number of purposes that may be quite narrow (such as a description of a single blood protein), or be quite wide, such as the nature of infectious diseases. Thus, they can be of the length of a book or just a few pages. Their lengths and nature thus depend on the purpose of the book if they are parts of such, but most of the time they are meant to stand in the world independently. Most of our review articles have been written for the purpose of summarizing the general topic of our research efforts, e.g., the physiology and chemistry of the blood protein transferrin, or the nature of certain microorganisms such as bifidobacteria. I personally wrote some such articles during the era of my research activities to simply summarize what we have done and perhaps to search for ideas on what to do in the future. So here goes:

1.) A. Bezkorovainy. Transferrin and the metabolism of iron. Rush-Presbyterian-St. Luke's Hospital Medical Bulletin 9:1-14, 1970. I wrote and published this article to acquaint the staff of the Hospital and Medical School where I worked in the lab. Besides teaching the medical students, that is.

2.) A. Bezkorovainy. Studies on the primary structure of human serum transferrin: a preliminary report. Ibid. 12:184-187, 1973. Purpose was basically the same as above.

3.) R. H. Zschocke and A. Bezkorovainy. Structure and function of transferrins. I. Physical, chemical, and iron-binding properties. Arzneimittel-Forschung 24:476-485, 1974. One of the reasons for writing this and the next article was to help my student, R. H. Zschocke to get a job in a German Pharmaceutical House as its research director. He was successful.

4.) R. H. Zschocke and A. Bezkorovainy. Structure and function of transferrins. II. Transferrin and iron metabolism. Arzneimittel-Forschung 24:726-737, 1974. The purpose was the same as that for No. 3.

5.) A. Bezkorovainy. Human milk and colostrums proteins. J. Dairy Science 60:1023=1037,1977. The purpose was to educate the dairy science and human milk experts on the benefits and composition of human milk.

6.) A. Bezkorovainy. Antimicrobial properties of iron-binding proteins. In "Diet and Resistance to Disease," edited by M. Phillips and A. L. Baez. Plenum Press, New York, pp.139-154, 1981. Invited chapter for a book.

7.) A. Bezkorovainy. Iron uptake by the microaerophilic anaerobe Bifidobacterium bifidum var. pennsylvanicus. Clinical Physiology and Biochemistry 2:291-297, 1984. Invitation by the newly organized Journal of Clinical Physiology and Biochemistry.

8.) A. Bezkorovainy. Iron Proteins. In "Iron and Infection," by J. J. Bullen and E. Griffiths, John Wiley and Sons, Ltd., 1987, pp. 27-67. Invited chapter included in the book.

9.) A. Bezkorovainy. Biochemistry of Non-heme iron in man. I. Iron proteins in cellular iron metabolism. Clinical Physiology and Biochemistry 7:1-17, 1989.

10.) A. Bezkorovainy. Biochemistry of Non-heme iron in man. II. Absorption of iron. Clinical Physiology and Biochemistry 7:53-69, 1989. Both# 9 and 10 were invited papers.

11.) A. Bezkorovainy, Eva Kot, Robin Miller-Catchpole, George Haloftis, and Sergey Furmanov. Iron metabolism in bifidobacteria. Internat. Dairy Journal 6:905-919, 1996. Invited article on iron metabolism in bifidobacteria.

12.) A. Bezkorovainy. Probiotics: determinants of survival and growth in the gut. Amer. J. Clin. Nutr. 73 (suppl.):3995-4005, 2001. Presented by A. Bezkorovainy at a symposium in Kiel, Germany, June 11-12, 1998.

PH. D. GRADUATES OF THE RUSH UNIVERSITY
BIOCHEMISTRY DEPARTMENT

This last section of Chapter 3 gives a brief review of how the Biochemistry Department received the right to award M. S. and Ph. D. degrees to its graduate students. We may recall that in the past, such degrees were granted only by the University of Illinois, though the students receiving such degrees may have earned them in the laboratories of Rush University under the direction of Rush medical and scientific staff. These staff were also on the unpaid faculty of the University of Illinois medical and graduate colleges, as a result of which the University of Illinois had the opportunity to accept quite a bit more students than it would have otherwise. Rush didn't have its own graduate college until the 1980's, though it had reestablished a medical school some 10 to 15 years before that. For that reason and especially for the purpose of running a first-rate hospital, Rush already had Departments of Pathology, Biochemistry, and Psychology that were already teaching Rush medical students; and for other basic medical school sciences such as physiology, anatomy, pharmacology, etc. it had faculty associated with other medical departments such as Internal Medicine. Rush could easily have established these non-existent departments if it decided to grant M. S. and Ph. D. degrees sooner. And they finally did; they only needed approval from the State of Illinois. The already existent Biochemistry Department tried to do it first. Our chairman was Dr. Howard Sky-Peck at that time, and he appointed a few of us Department of Biochemistry members to prepare for the state committee's visit. And guess who was on that committee: all were faculty members from the University of Illinois Medical College. One of them was especially hostile towards me; he complained that I had a law degree and with two professions, I would not be able to do a good job teaching graduate students, even though I was already doing it. The other reason, I believe, was because I took Bill Line (see above) as my student after he had a quarrel with his Illinois professor and had to leave his laboratory. I was expected to refuse him and Bill Line would have been kicked out of Illinois Graduate College for not being able to be accepted by a graduate college professor to sponsor his dissertation work. But Bill Line turned out to be a good biochemist, and I don't know if there would have been Miller's light beer in our world, if I hadn't accepted him. God bless his soul! So the State of Illinois committee refused to allow us to grant graduate degrees. Poor Dr. Sky-Peck became ill, resigned his department chairmanship, and a search committee (of which I was a member) appointed Dr. Kuettner as the Department of Biochemistry chairman. Soon enough, he arranged to invite another state committee to allow us to grant Ph. D. degrees (Dr. Kuettner insisted that no University of Illinois professor be a member), and they found no issues to criticize us, and, in fact, they greatly praised our competence to choose and train graduate students. We were approved to award M. S. and Ph. D. degrees. The other basic science departments followed after they were properly organized.

Our first graduate student to receive the Ph. D. degree in biochemistry was Dr. Nancy Topouzian, who was my student and left Rush with some half a dozen publications based on her dissertation. She had been an RN nurse before her marriage to Dr. Leo Topouzian, who was a Orthopedics surgery resident in the hospital where she was working. After she raised her family, she went to graduate school at Rush and majored in biochemistry. She graduated from Rush in 1985 and got a postdoctoral job at Evanston Hospital-Northwestern University, where she tried to solve the problem of the Armenian Disease, which is a genetic disease similar to that of Parkinson's. It hits largely Middle Eastern populations, of which her husband's family had originated. Nancy published some papers on the biochemistry associated with the disease, but like other numerous scientists, could not find a cure. She then accepted a job at the Loyola University Nursing College teaching biochemistry to its students.

And so, after our Biochemistry Department was given the rights to award Ph. D. degrees, I was appointed by our department chair to run that graduate program in addition to my other duties. Because of that, I was not looking for graduate students to do research on matters of my interests, and so, before I retired, I had only 3 additional graduate students in addition to Nancy Topouzian. And one of them, Robin Miller-catchpole, M. D. received her Ph. D. post mortem, and I did not have much effort with her degree. So it wasn't too hard to "maintain order" in the department while Dr. Kuettner was traveling around the country raising funds for his department, or managing his plentiful graduate students doing research in bone biochemistry. But let me return to Dr. Miller-Catchpole; I mentioned above that she started visiting our department when she was a medical student. She was much interested in research and in her "free time" she participated in helping my associates with my research. She received her MD degree, did her residency in pathology, then worked, and then decided to get a Ph.

D. degree in biochemistry. She entered the very department that already knew her and welcomed her. She did some work on lactoferrin and its donation of iron for the growth of Bifidobacterium breve, but before graduating, she acquired a malignant disease and passed away. I had her research results published, and requested the administration to grant her a post mortem Ph. D. degree. The administration agreed, and Robin Miller-Catchpole can now be mentioned with M. D., Ph. D. degrees with her name. God bless her soul, and many thanks to the Rush administration for granting her the final degree.

Another of my last students was Mark Poch, a young man from Wisconsin, who stayed with me for some 5 years and got his name on 5 papers, with his first ones on two of them. He was from Wisconsin and returned to his home by taking a job in Milwaukee, as I recall. His two principal papers were the following: "Growth enhancing supplements for various species of bifidobacteria." J. Dairy Science 71:3214, 1988 and "Bovine milk k-casein trypsin digest is growth enhancer for Genus Bifidobacterium," J. of Agricultural and Food Chemistry 39:73, 1991. And the last graduate student I had was Xianwen Yi, who was from China and spent only 1 to 1.5 years working in my lab. I already mentioned him above.

Last but not least, I had worked with technicians, who were superb chemists; they did what I was directing them to do, which often was to use their own views and opinions. I put our technicians' names on practically all publications that they had something to do with. I already mentioned Dr. Dietmar Grohlich, who earned his Ph. D. with me in 1979, and who for many years was working as a "technician" with me. Then there was Eva Kot, M. S., a graduate of University of Illinois in Urbana, who replaced Dietmar Grohlich when the latter obtained his Ph. D. degree and left Rush. She worked with me for many years and retired when I did. Her name is on many of our publications, including papers with several authors such as Robin Miller-Catchpole, Eva Kot, George Haloftis, Sergey Furmanov, and Anatoly Bezkorovainy, Nutrition Research 17:205-213, 1997, and sometimes, papers with her name first, e.g., Eva Kot and Anatoly Bezkorovainy, "Distribution of accumulated iron in Bifidobacterium thermophilum," Journal of Agricultural and Food Chemistry 41:177, 1993, or Eva Kot, Sergey Furmanov, and Anatoly Bezkorovainy, "Accumulation of iron in lactic acid bacteria and bifidobacteria," Journal of Food Science 60:547, 1995. These papers, as well as several others, carry the name of Sergey Furmanov, who worked with me while he was studying pre-medical curriculum at the neighboring University of Illinois. He was a Russian immigrant, who had already been attending a medical school in Russia when his parents decided to emigrate to the U.S. Ms. Eva Kot thought that he was the smartest individual in our research group (she probably included me in that bunch). After Furmanov had graduated from the University of Illinois, he was accepted at Rush Medical College and became a medical student. He is now practicing medicine in the Chicago area.

Another young man and hopeful medical student who worked with us in the 1990's was George Haloftis, who was born in Greece but was very young when he came to the U. S. He too wanted to get into our Medical school, but was unsuccessful. He was accepted at the Tucson, Arizona Osteopathic School and is now practicing medicine as well, though I don't know where. He too was a co-author on several of our publications, e. g., "Iron metabolism in Bifidobacteria," by Anatoly Bezkorovainy, Eva Kot, Robin Miller-Catchpole, George Haloft is, and Sergey Furmanov, International Dairy Journal 6:905, 1996.

I retired from full time work at Rush in the year of 2000, however, for another 5 years (until I was 70 years old) I remained on Rush's payroll on a part-time basis. The last research paper we published was authored by Eva Kot and Anatoly Bezkorovainy, titled "Effect of Al (III) on surface properties of Bifidobacterium thermophilum as a function of temperature," Biological Trace Element Research, 86:159, 2002. I never published any research papers thereafter, though that does not include non science books. I remained at Rush for another 5 years after I "retired" in 2000 A. D., teaching graduate and medical students at Rush Medical College and the Chicago College of Podiatric Medicine. In 2005 A.D. My wife and I moved from Lincolnwood to Galena, Illinois, where we expected to remain for the rest of our lives. But it did not happen so: in about 2010, Marilyn was diagnosed with Parkinson's Disease, and in 2015, i.e., after 10 years in Galena, Illinois, we had to move to Arizona because Marilyn could no longer climb the stairs to our bedroom in our house. We sold our Galena house in that year and moved to Sun Lakes, Arizona (a "suburb" of Chandler), where we already had a single storey house without a basement or attic since 2010 and where we used to spend our winters since then. Our son Alex, a history teacher at a local high school, was already living in Chandler for almost 20 years, and my cousin Nora had been living there for some 35 years. But we still hated to leave Galena, Illinois, and our life in Arizona is a different story: spending 4 months a year was enough.

CHAPTER 4

THE RUSH-PRESBYTERIAN-ST, LUKE'S MEDICAL CENTER

The first three chapters of this book are concerned with my (the author's) young life in Europe (1935- 1951), then in Wilkes-Barre, Pennsylvania (1951), then in Chicago (1951-1960), and Oak Ridge, Tennessee, Ames, Iowa, and back to Chicago in 1962. At this time, at my age of Sf years, as I look back at my life, including spending 9 years of it going to schools (2 years in high school, 3 years in college, and 4 year fin graduate school), I was often wandering if such a long while of schooling was worth it; most of my DP friends that I had from my church and other sources finished high schools and then went to work, usually marrying fellow immigrant girls in their early 20's. I was 29 when I was married (1964), only a couple years younger than when my dad had married my mom, but he earlier had a wife, a Latvian woman, whom he married at the age of 21 in order to get out of Soviet Russia into the independent Latvia, where she died of tuberculosis a few years later. My dad was a medical student in Russia when he left it, but he never continued his studies in Latvia. My brother was married at the age of 26 after he received his MS degree in engineering at the University of Illinois. So both of us were never "unemployed," like our father was so often and was dependent on my mother's earnings with her beauty culture profession or my brother's and my helpings.

I managed to complete my work toward a BS degree in 3 years, in part by going to school in summers instead of playing ball with other fellow students on the Atlantic shores of Florida. And when I was already in graduate school, I was receiving a small but significant salary for teaching biochemistry to medical students with which I could help my parents. It wasn't an easy or pleasant life when I was a student, but it paid me high rewards during and after my further life, especially after I married my wife and raised two kids with her, who also received super educations useful for: the rest of their lives. But getting back to when I started graduate school, I have to start by stating that I had never expected to get such an education. My father was pushing me toward medicine, since he himself was an unfinished medical student in his youth, and now he wanted his son to be a doctor, He never thought how I would pay for the tuition and other expenses for an extra four years in a medical school; if you are a medical student, you don't have time to get a part-time job; those medical courses take a huge amount of time, and I wasn't smart enough to both earn tuition and food payments and learn the complex subjects of the medical profession. But at first I followed my father's "advice;" I applied to the University of Illinois medical school; there are 5 other medical schools in Chicago; but they are private, and their tuition is fantastic (I could have never afforded them). And the University of Illinois would have been the only one I could have afforded to attend. I applied, and was called for an interview, which I flunked badly. My interviewer asked me what I would want to do as a doctor. I told him what I learned at the University of Chicago: to cure diseases that are still not curable like Parkinson's Disease or all the cancers in our world. This is basically what we were taught at the University of Chicago; the stupid me, I truly wanted to do medical research and cure diseases that were yet incurable. But this is not what the University of Illinois interviewer wanted to hear: he told me that they wanted to train doctors to go to Southern Illinois, where there was a shortage of doctors, and there I would practice medicine in the rural villages and small towns there. The interviewer was a good guy; he saw I was disappointed and he said to me that he will call the chairman of the biochemistry department and send me to him to get accepted for the Ph. D. in a biochemistry program so that I can learn how to do research to cure, for instance, cancer. I was admitted then and there to the graduate school of the University of Illinois, with a scholarship of $2000/year and no tuition or other payment demands, and I started graduate school immediately after I received my degree of BS in biochemistry from University of Chicago in that fall of 1956. That was the end of my attempt to major in medicine and an unexpected admission to the Biochemistry Department for a study toward the Ph. D. degree. My professor with whom I would do my dissertation was Dr. Richard Winzler, head of the University of Illinois Department of Biochemistry, with whom I studied in the next 4 years, until 1960, when I finished all the work necessary for a Ph. D. degree, and in September of 1960, I left Chicago to Oak Ridge National Laboratory for post-doctoral training. They were paying me $6600 per year (the biggest salary that I had ever made). The official degree of Ph. D. was officially awarded to me in May of 1961.

My professor, Dr. Richard Winzler, was at the University of Illinois for about 2 years before I got there in 1956. He was a good administrator; probably he got the University of Illinois Biochemistry Department chairmanship because of his discovery of the possibly most acidic plasma protein which he called orosomucoid. It was visible by paper electrophoresis at pH 4.5 of human plasma on the positive end of the paper strip toward the positive end. The protein still had a negative charge at that pH; in fact, it was the most negatively charged protein at pH 4.5 as far as we are aware. Most plasma proteins had a net positive charge and moved to the negative pole. This was due to the fact that it had a huge amount of sialic acid in its structure (total carbohydrate amount is 40%, the rest are amino acids). No one knew what it was doing in human serum, but its level was increased when the patient had an infectious disease. Normally, at pH 8.6, the electrophoretic position of this protein was the alpha-1 territory, and at electrophoresis at pH 4.5, it moved to the positive pole as fast as it did at pH 8.6 (alpha- 1 position). If the sialic acid was removed from orosomucoid (it was possible to do with a very weak acidity), the protein acquired a positive net charge at pH 4.5 and moved with serum albumin and most other proteins in an electrophoresis apparatus. At pH 4.5, serum electrophoresis of blood plasma showed, in addition to orosomucoid (alpha-1 territory), a slower moving protein(s), also still negative but not as seriously as orosomucoid was. I was supposed to investigate that group of proteins for my Ph. D. degree. It was called the M-2 group, while orosomucoid was of the M-1 group.

For my Ph. D. thesis, I isolated a protein of that M-2 group; it had about 20% carbohydrate as opposed to orosomucoid's 40%, and had a different molecular weight. Electrophoretically, at pH 4.5, it moved also to the positive pole but slower than orosomucoid, thus it was an alpha-2 rather than alpha-1 protein. We published a paper on this protein (Bezkorovainy, A. and Winzler, R. J. Biochim. Biophys. Acta 49:559-565, 1961), but we could not compare the amino acid analyses because our department did not have an amino acid analysis apparatus. Its molecular weight appeared to be similar to that of orosomucoid, but we could not know for sure because we again did not have an ultracentrifuge in our laboratory. Thus, we graduate students of the University of Illinois, could not obtain a lot of information on proteins because we didn't have the appropriate instrumentaTIon necessary therefor in the department; many biochemistry departments in the pre-1960's did not have many appropriate instruments necessary to do important research activities, but thankfully, Biochimica et Biophysica Acta published our paper without necessary and desired information; and I got my Ph. D. degree in addition!

So when I went to the Oak Ridge National Laboratory for my postdoctoral work, my boss there, Dr. Dave Doherty, suggested that I work on platelet biochemistry (platelets are blood cells of much smaller size than red blood cells) that are essential for the blood coagulation process, and I had to get a supply of them to do some work on them. There was amazingly little information about the biological nature of blood platelets, and to study them, I had to find a source of them so I could do some biochemical work on them. Oak Ridge Laboratory had no place where I could find human platelets; in fact, there was no place where I could get human blood and then isolate platelets from it. I decided to work on bovine platelets, because I could get plenty of bovine blood and isolate platelets therefrom, which turned out to be an unusually hard process; it was much harder to get bovine platelets from bovine blood than human platelets from human one. But I learned the process and had sufficient amounts of bovine platelets to study them (incidentally, the bovine platelets seemed to be smaller than human ones and to separate them from the red cells was much harder than from the human blood). We did not find much interesting stuff in the bovine platelets: there was some hemoglobin there, large amounts of fibrinogen, and some serum albumin, but little if any of other normal plasma proteins. We checked for enzyme activities, and found some, but nothing exceptional (Bezkorovainy, A. and Doherty, D. G. Archives Biochem. Biophys. 86:412, 1962). When I moved to Rush in 1962, I prepared human platelets from human blood and did similar work on the human as we did on bovine platelets. There was not much of a difference (Bezkorovainy, A. and Rafelson, M. E. Characterization of some proteins from human platelets. J. Lab. Clin. Med. 64:212, 1964). In Oak Ridge, preparing the blood platelets for analysis, we had left a huge amount of bovine plasma that we didn't bother to use; that is, my boss wanted to throw it out. I decided to use it; I hated to just throw out bovine plasma. I isolated several grams of the bovine orosomucoid glycoprotein from it and did an analysis. I didn't find too much of a difference between the bovine serum and human serum orosomucoid after I isolated and purified the two. We published a paper in the British journal Nature (Bezkorovainy, A. and Doherty, D. G. Comparative study of bovine and human orosomucoide. Nature 195:1003, 1962). There was little if any difference between them, but our little paper was quite popular in our biochemical community, for some reason.

In summer of 1961, after a year at Oak Ridge, Tenn. Laboratory, I decided to leave Tennessee and join the National Animal Disease Laboratory that was organized and built in Ames, Iowa, and which had a large group of veterinarians and a small group of Ph. D. biochemists, who were supposed to be in aid of the veterinarians in their attempts to develop cures of animal diseases. They offered me a permanent job at the GS-12 level with a salary of $8900/year (my boss was GS-13). That was a nice civil service job, good conditions and pay (I had a separate office and a lab), and the lab had an ultracentrifuge which could be used for protein molecular weight determinations and hardly any of their workers were using it. In Oak Ridge, I had to wait at least a month before I could use the ultracentrifuge to determine a protein's molecular weight, and at University of Illinois we never had one. And when they accepted me for work there, they said that I would be appointed Assistant or Associate Professor at the Iowa State University which was located also in Ames, and if I wanted, I could participate in teaching veterinary profession students. So, I left Oak Ridge and moved "lock, stock, and barrel" to Ames, Iowa. I was now 300 miles from Chicago where my parents lived, and the girl that I liked (named Marilyn) also lived. It took 5 hours to get to Chicago from Ames, whereas from Oak Ridge it took 2 days. I became quite friendly with most of the folks, including the other 5 members of the Biochemistry Department, the leader of which was Dr. Roepke, a former professor of the University of Minnesota. My colleagues were all friendly chaps, all Ph. D. men, who most of their time at work were sitting at their desks presumably planning their research work after their move from Bethesda, Maryland (I think I remember that their laboratories were located there before their move to Ames, Iowa). I was used, however, to work in the laboratory, and plan my experiments at home, so I started doing experiments after ordering chemicals and glassware that I needed, and by George, that lab had just about everything I needed for doing my protein work. So I started working right away, and I published I think some 2 papers in one year, which are the following: A. Bezkorovainy. Some physical and chemical properties of an M-2 glycoprotein isolated from bovine plasma. Biochemistry 2:10-16, 1963; A. Bezkorovainy. Monosaccharides of bovine acid glycoproteins. Arch. Biochem. Biophys. 101:66-70, 1963. I think I published a couple more, but I could not find them.

In Ames, Iowa I stayed only a year. I was never given a professorial position (unsalaried) at the Iowa State University, which they promised. I got involved with my future wife Marilyn more seriously than I was before, and I wanted to be living closer to her, and I missed my relatives and friends as I got older. So I decided to move back to Chicago, and in the fall of 1962, I did so. I figured that 2 years away from "home" was enough, and in addition, my former professor became the chairman of the Biochemistry Department at Rush-Presbyterian-St. Luke's Hospital, which was expecting to reactivate Rush Medical College in the future and they were building the group of professors that would start the new medical school. And that's what I really wanted to be eventually; a professor, and Rush-Presbyterian-St. Luke's organization was to me a most likely candidate for such a future (and it really happened, but not right away). Though Rush was not an independent medical school (but eventually it became one), its Ph. D. employees were allowed to teach at University of Illinois, and we even, as unpaid professors, had the right to accept graduate MS and Ph. D. students, who were permitted to work for their dissertations at the laboratories of Rush-Presbyterian-St. Luke's Medical Center under the leadership of Rush employees (and University of Illinois Professors). As I entered the Rush environment for work, University of Illinois gave me the title of Assistant Professor (in the Biochemistry Department) so I could have and train graduate students who would get their MS or Ph. D. degrees from the University of Illinois but do their degree work at Rush.

I had 10 students that got their Ph. D.'s under my leadership since I came to work at Rush in 1962. At first, the Ph. D.'s were awarded by the University of Illinois since many of us Rush-Presbyterian-St. Luke's Hospital employees were also professors at the University of Illinois. Later, in the 1970's, after we set up the Rush Medical College and established the Rush University, we received our own rights to award the Ph. D. and M. S. degrees to our students. Of course, we could not send our students to University of Illinois to take courses in their graduate programs, but we now had our own medical school and our graduate students now could take their basic courses with their medical students, e.g., in biochemistry. Our graduate students took the same medical biochemistry courses as the medical students did, and as electives, they could take any basic science course(s) as they wanted which the medical students were taking, e. g., physiology or pharmacology. The advanced biochemistry courses, we, of course, had to teach separately by ourselves (e.g., enzymology, carbohydrate chemistry, or biochemical laboratory techniques (ultracentrifuge usage, anyone?). For instance, I was teaching a course in protein chemistry for graduate students, and I even wrote a book for that purpose (A. Bezkorovainy, "Basic Protein Chemistry," Charles Thomas, Publ., Springfield, IL, 1970, 231 pp.). To take such advanced biochemistry courses, the graduate students had to have taken basic medical school biochemistry, which lasted for 2 quarters and was also taken by all medical students. My colleague and former chairman Dr. Max Rafelson had written with Drs. James Hayashi and Steve Binkley a small biochemistry book, perhaps for review purposes by medical students, and that was in the 1960's. After that, there were the second and third editions of "Basic Biochemistry" published out there, and in 1979, I was invited by Dr. Rafelson to participate in publishing the "Fourth Edition" of the book, I assume because their third author had retired. I joined them, and "Basic Biochemistry" Fourth Edition was published by Macmillan publisher in 1980. The book was used quite a lot by medical students while taking the course, but also for reviewing biochemistry materials before taking the mid-term (post sophomore) medical student overall examination. It had 415 pages, quite a few more than the previous editions. What can be considered the fifth and last edition of the book, was published in 1996; it had some 600 pages and could no longer be called a review book. It was authored by Anatoly Bezkorovainy and Max E. Rafelson; Dr. Hayashi had retired and did not participate. And it could no longer be called a review book too, but in no way could it be compared to the newest biochemistry textbook by Thomas Deviin's "Textbook of Biochemistry," with 1200 pages, Wiley-Liss Publisher (6th edition), 2006. After our last book with 400+ pages, neither Dr. Rafelson nor I attempted to write a book that would compete with the Devlin's master-job. The only thing we can do is to congratulate Professor Thomas Devlin for a job perfectly done.

I had a total of 10 graduate students who received their Ph. D.'s with me. In addition, I had students whom I was directing in their research progress because their professors didn't have enough time to spend with them, like, e. g., in my case there was Dr. Tohru Inouye who was often training me when Dr. Winzler, my professor was often too busy or out of town. One such student who was basically trained by me was Dr. Rafelson officially, but I was often her advisor when her boss was busy. Her name was Claire Gerbeck, who was officially Dr. Rafelson's student, but I was often her advisor and instructor. And Dr. Rafelson was very honest: the authors of papers published from Dr. Gerbeck's journal articles included my name: Gerbeck, Rafelson, and Bezkorovainy, Biochim. Biophys. Acta 101:229, 1965 and Gerbeck, Bezkorovainy, and Rafelson, Biochemistry 6:403, 1967. The next graduate student I want to mention was Bill line (he was a former U.S. army veteran), whom I met after he got into some issues with his professor at the University of Illinois. I don't know what the problem was, but his professor was simply not easy to get along with. Bill asked me if he could become my student and I accepted him. He was a good researcher, he stayed with me for some 2 years, and we could publish 2 good papers based on the results of his work: Line, W. F., Bezkorovainy, A., and Grohlich, D. Effect of chemical modification on the iron-binding properties of human transferrin. Biochemistry 6:3393-3402, 1967; and Line, W. F., Sly, D. A., and Bezkorovainy, A. Limited cleavage of human lactoferrin with pepsin. Intern. J. Biochem. 7:203-208, 1976. The Biochemistry paper was especially powerful because it showed which transferrin side-chains were binding the iron. Bill line had a successful work result with Milwaukee's Miller Beer Company: he was one of the employees who found out how to make "light beers" (low calories), and when he retired, he had a great feast day at his employer's place in Milwaukee, Wisconsin. Unfortunately, Dr. Bill Line passed away not too long after his retirement feast day, God bless his soul!

The smartest graduate student I had, in my opinion, was Reiner Zschocke. He had a chemical bachelor's degree, but I don't remember from where: Germany or the U.S. He was from Germany and came to the U. S. to get doctorate education. He had contact with a German chemical company, and they had apparently told him to get a doctorate and then come back to take over the company's research efforts. In this country (America) he met a German young lady and the two of them got married. The German lady wanted to go back to Germany, but Reiner seemed to like America and was not in a hurry to go back. But he had applied and got accepted at the University of Illinois graduate school, and entered as a graduate student into our Biochemistry Department. He chose me as his professor, perhaps because he knew Dietmar Grohlich, my technician, who was also from Germany. After a year, I considered him as the smartest individual in our student group. His dissertation was superb, and during his tenure as a student, we published 3 research papers and two review articles: A. Bezkorovainy and R. Zschocke. Structure and function of transferrins. I. Physical, chemical and iron binding properties. Arzneimittel-Forschung 24:476-485, 1974. Zschocke, R. and A. Bezkorovainy. Structure and function of transferrins. II. Transferrin and iron metabolism. Arzneimittel-Forschung 24:726-737, 1974. Zschocke, R.H. and A. Bezkorovainy. Some immunochemical properties of succinylated human transferrin and related proteins. Biochim. Biophys. Acta 200:241246, 1970. Zschocke, R. H. and A. Bezkorovainy. The function of amino groups in the binding of iron by transferrin. Eur. J. Biochem. 25:147-152, 1972. Bezkorovainy, A. Zschocke, R. H. and D. Grohlich. Some physical chemical properties of succinylated transferrin, conalbumin, and orosomucoid. Biochim. Biophys. Acta 181:295-304,1969. Reiner Zschocke received his doctorate and went back to Germany with his happy wife and a child, and was appointed head of the research unit of a German drug company: a strong and powerful research position among a drug company population. But a couple years later, we got sudden information that Reiner Zschocke had killed himself. He had apparently gone to a scientific meeting outside the city where he worked in Germany and shot himself (I was surprised to hear that he had a gun with him; these are not as easy to own in Germany as they are in the U.S.). Why he did it, we don't know. He apparently did not leave a note. God bless his soul.

Not too long after Dr. Reiner Zschocke left us to Germany, I acquired another brilliant worker, who achieved a great success after he left my laboratory, like Dr. Zschocke; but he did not kill himself and acquired a tremendous success in his life after he left my lab. His name was (and is) Jim Nichols, Ph. D., who received his Ph. D. in biochemistry from Northwestern University and started working for Dr. Georg Springer as a postdoctoral fellow at the Evanston Hospital (this hospital is connected to Northwestern University). But Dr. Springer all of a sudden ran out of money (I suspect that he didn't get a grant from either the U.S. government or another source that he expected to get). He called me and asked if I could help; he might have already told about his problem to Dr. Nichols (who had a family), and who had already applied for a job at the U.S. post office and was ready to get started there. I was surprised that he could not get a job in his doctoral profession (perhaps because he was black?). I happened to have some grant money which could employ a postdoctoral fellow for a couple years, and I grabbed Dr. Nichols. He was a well-trained biochemist (Northwestern University produces good scientists) and I was not disappointed; in a couple of years in my lab, he did enough work to organize four publications with his name on them: Nichols, J. H., Bezkorovainy, A., and Paque, R. Isolation and characterization of several glycoproteins from human colostrum whey. Biochim. Biophys. Acta 412:99-108, 1975; Nichols, J.H. and Bezkorovainy, A. Isolation and characterization of several glycoproteins from human colostrum whey. Biochim. Biophys. Acta 412:99-108, 1975; by Bezkorovainy, A., D. A. Sly, and J. H. Nichols. J. Biochem. 7:639-645, 1976; Bezkorovainy, A.

and Nichols, J. H. Glycoproteins of mature human milk, Pediatric Research 10:1-5, 1976; Bezkorovainy, A., Grohlich, D., and Nichols, J. H. Isolation of a glycopeptide fraction with Lactobacillus bifidus var. penn. growth-promoting activity from whole human milk casein. Amer. J. Clin. Nutr. 32:1428-1432, 1969. Dr. Jim Nichols in his spare time was helping black medical students to pass my biochemistry course, being quite successful at that, and he finally decided that he too wants to go to medical school. He applied to Rush, I wrote an excellent resume, and he was accepted at Rush Medical School. In four years he received his M. D. degree and went on to do human medicine. I excused him from taking our biochemistry course, and he spent his free time by helping other black students, to whom, for some reason, biochemistry was very difficult. That year, not a single black student flunked biochemistry. But after he graduated, I lost contact with him, except that once in a while I would get a letter from one of his helpers to send him something that he needed to get from our authorities. Most recently, I got a letter from a Chicago college that Dr. Nichols had retired from practicing medicine and got a job as professor of biochemistry at a Chicago college; and he wanted me to send copies of his publications to his new college authorities. I am sure he will succeed as a college teacher just as he succeeded by being a doctor. Just think: how much more did Dr. Nichols do for human beings by being a physician and professor opposed to working at the post office that he was expecting to do in his youth? Thank God for what he has achieved!

In my working years, I had a few post-doctoral fellows working with me, 11ke Dr. Jim Nichols, even though I never advertised such positions being open for recent Ph. D. graduates. But it so happened that I have had several of them, and they were all exceptionally smart and successful. One of them was Dr. D. A. Sly, a quiet but smart Ph. D. woman, who wanted to learn more on how to be a Ph. D. researcher before acquiring a permanent position somewhere. She published a couple of papers as the first author and published also a couple book chapters with me as authors: D. A. Sly and A. Bezkorovainy. A carboxyl-terminal amino acid of human serum transferrin. Physiol. Chem. & Physics 6:171-177, 1974; same authors: Transferrin in reticulocyte cytosol. Biochim. Biophys. Acta 385:36-41, 1975; Bezkorovainy, A., Grohlich, D., and Sly, D. A. Cleavage of human transferrin with N bromosuccinimide. Int. J. Protein and Peptide Res. 8:291-293, 1975. The book chapters were in R.H. Chrichton's "Proteins of Iron Storage and Transport," and R. E. Harmon's "Cell Surface Carbohydrate Chemistry." I also had a postdoctoral fellow from an Arabic country Dr. S. Ibrahim, who published his work in his own country's journals: S. Ibrahim and A. Bezkorovainy: J. Food Science 59:189-192; J. Food Protection 56:713-715, 1993; and J. of Science of Food Agriculture 62:351-354, 1993. His journals were unknown to me, but they were obviously active in their field.

My maximum publisher worker was Eva Kot, M. S., who worked as a coworker and co:.publisher with me. I-fer name was most likely No. 2 among our publication authors, with mine as Numero Uno. She was a Polish immigrant, with an MS degree from the University of Illinois; I often offered her to enter our university and work for me for a doctorate degree; I was convinced that she would have done a perfect job with it. But her husband was a Ph. D. in physics and apparently she thought that one per family was enough. She worked with me for 20+ years and retired when I did in the year of 2000 A. D.

Another helper of mine over a number of years was Dietmar Grohlich, a German immigrant who knew Dr. Zschocke, but got into the Ph. D. area somewhat later, in the late 1970's. He began working with me as a technician pretty much when I started working at Rush around 1964. He was a good technician and I used his name on our papers as a co-worker. He was also attending the University of Illinois in Chicago and eventually received a BS in chemistry; and on a part-time basis, he entered the University of Illinois' Medical College Pathology Department's Ph. D. graduate program. Illinois gives Ph. D. degrees in pathology; you don't have to go to medical school to get that degree; they train you in the art of handling diseases in the laboratory by inventing drugs or other medical care. Dietmar entered their program, took pathology courses with the medical students, and advanced courses in other subjects, and to get a Ph. D. degree in pathology, he had to do a research project with a pathology professor. So guess what: in order to do that, he asked his pathology department chair to give me a non-salaried position as Professor of University of Illinois Pathology Department, and as such, I now had the right to have Dietmar Grohlich as my Ph. D. graduate student. And he did a good job with that: we published two papers on his research project: Grohlich and Bezkorovainy: Biochemical Research Communications 76:682-690, 1977; and International Journal of Biochemistry 10:787-802, 1979. He received his Ph. D. degree from University of Illinois' Pathology Department, and they accepted Dietmar right away in a leadership position of the State of Illinois Forensic Laboratory organization. He worked there running forensic works for the State of Illinois until his retirement somewhere after the year of 2000. He also married his girlfriend sometime around when he received his Ph. D. degree, and they had a daughter to whom I was her God-father in a Roman-Catholic Church. Dietmar retired from his state job sometime between 2005 and 2010, and moved to Florida with his wife, who soon thereafter passed away. His daughter became a nurse, got married, and still resides with her family in Deerfield, Illinois. Every summer, to get away from Florida heat, Dietmar goes north to stay with her daughter's family, and before we moved to Arizona, we had always met with him during these summer times.

And for a next event, I want to mention another student of mine of whom I am quite proud of: Nancy Topouzian. Her original profession has been nursing, and she met Dr. Leo Topouzian (an Armenian Orthodox man from Egypt), whose parents had escaped from Turkey to Egypt during World War I. Dr. Leo had become a physician in France, and emigrated to the U.S. He was an orthopedic resident in a Chicago hospital where the future Nancy Topouzian was a nurse. The doctor married the nurse, a son was soon born, and the Topouzians rented a larger apartment in a building owned by Marilyn's (my future wife's) parents. And that's where I had met the Topouzian family. We became good friends; Leo Topouzian soon finished his residency, began his practice, bought a house in Skokie, Illinois (suburb of Chicago), which was not too far from my wife's and my house in Lincolnwood. So we were good friends as our kids were growing up. As Leo got older, he got interested in what he called the Armenian disease, which is similar to Parkinson's disease, but for some reason, it attacks and kills largely Armenians. So he decided that Nancy should get a Ph. D. degree and get into a research activity to invent a cure of the Armenian disease. And furthermore, I should organize this project. I said to Leo "OK," get some forms, fill them out, and send them to our Rush University admissions committee, and I'll handle the rest. Well, Nancy was a good nursing student, a good nurse, and was admitted to the Biochemistry Department of Rush University. There were some issues because Rush was requesting the State of Illinois to allow it to give Ph. D. degrees in biochemistry and other medical subjects at Rush; but all issues were eventually cleared up. Nancy did a good job as a graduate student, and received the Ph.D. degree in biochemistry; in fact this was the first Ph.D. degree that Rush University Medical College was allowed to give to its doctoral students by the State. She was actually the first Ph.D. that Rush University had ever awarded. She got some 5 publications papers from her doctoral thesis, and was accepted as a research professor at the Northwestern University-Evanston Hospital, where Nancy attempted to master the Armenian Disease (of course at the urging of her husband). After some 3 years she was able to publish a paper on that disease, but no major results on that disease were discovered by her. Nancy then left to Loyola Medical College where she taught biochemistry to nursing students, and after some years she retired with a Loyola pension.

So the Armenian Disease was not conquered; we have to wait for some other super biochemist to do the job. And some 10+ years after Nancy tried, nobody else was more successful.

In my work at Rush for some 38 years, I have trained some 10 Ph.D. students, plus at least 5 post-doctoral fellows. I have described a few excellent ones, though all of them were superb biochemists, who published several papers with me, and received superb jobs after they left me. Some went to medical schools, and a Ph.D. degree in biochemistry will be of great help for them. May God bless them and their professional lives their professional lives, perhaps with a Nobel Prize? God bless perhaps with one or two Nobel Prizes??

Over the years, perhaps since the 1980's, we traveled for pleasure and otherwise through many countries, mostly European, of which we were interested in. Many were in connection with Anatoly's job, giving papers at various scientific meetings and symposia. Our travels to Russia were somewhat different; no one had invited Anatoly to give papers at symposia or seminars at scientific meetings in Russia. The reasons were religious and chauvinistic. Russia was the country where our ancestors came from. And much of Russian culture came from other European origins, preceding Russia for thousands of years such as Greece, Rome, and Palestine (even though Palestine is not in Europe, ideas originating from there, as e.g., Christianity, were very influential in Europe). Though we tried to get to Palestine, we did not succeed, unfortunately; closest to that was Egypt. If we had another 50+ years to live, we would undoubtedly have visited Asia and Africa (beyond Egypt). But since the human life span consists only of 70-80 years, such additional travels were impossible to accomplish. Even in Europe, we missed a lot, e. g., Spain and Portugal and their American descendants like Brazil, Mexico, and South- and Mid-American lands, though I did have a chance to visit Argentina and Belize, once each but that's not enough. And even the Belize culture is less Spanish/South American than it is British.

The style of traveling that we chose was the easiest one: we would fly to Europe, then board a tourist ship that would take us to the various countries that we had chosen to see previously. And then, as the ship was visiting the appropriate ports, we could choose to either leave the ship and visit the stopped area, or, if not interested, we could stay aboard and enjoy all the ship's creature comforts. That's how we did the trip to the Baltic states in the year 2000, described in chapter 3 herein, though the ships in these later trips, usually Mediterranean ones, were quite a bit larger, around 40,000 tons rather than the 4000-ton boat we traveled on in the Baltic Sea. We used mostly the Renaissance Cruises company for these travels. As I recall, we visited Southern and Eastern Europe, and part of the Middle East about four times, I don't remember exactly how many, so we saw several places such as Istanbul at least two times. So I cannot accurately coordinate dates with places; all I can tell my readers is that we visited these profoundly interesting areas over a period of a few years, between the years of 1999 and 2005 (?), about the same period of time when we were also visiting Russia.

And so, as I recall, our first lengthy trip to Europe, unconnected with my job, was in 1999, about a year before I retired from full time work at Rush University. We visited Greece, Turkey, and some other areas. The most memorable event occurred when we were staying in the Renaissance Hotel in Istanbul and we were hit by an earthquake at night. We were told to evacuate (via stairs, no elevators) and to camp in a hotel hall until we were allowed to go back. There were only minor damages to the building, but a store on the first floor suffered some serious losses. The center of the earthquake was near Ankara (capital of Turkey), where they had losses of lives and serious damages. But from Istanbul, we could not call our home in Chicago and tell our kids that we were all OK. But we could send a telegram, which we did. Illustrations show the protective wall of the city of Constantinople, as Istanbul was called in its Byzantium times, when it was captured by the Turks in 1452-1453 A. D., ending the existence of the Byzantium kingdom, after a siege of only two months or so. It is surprising how flimsy that wall looks. No wonder the Turks captured the city so rapidly. Compared to the nature of Russian monastery walls such as those of Tikhvin's or Sergiev Posad (mentioned in the previous chapter), they were pretty miserly; no wonder the Russians could withstand sieges by Western invader armies (Poles and Swedes) for months if not years until help arrived either from Heaven (Tikhvin) or the Russian tsar. Constantinople became Istanbul after it was captured by the Turks, and that is what it is called today. It acquired its name of Constantinople in 326 A. D. Rome's Cesar Constantine chose to move the capital of the Roman Empire from Rome to a Roman town on Bosporus Straits called Byzantium. And from that point on, the former Roman Empire was called the Byzantine Empire with Constantinople as its capital. It lasted for some 1100 years.

While Rome of the former Roman Empire was practically in trouble all the time in the Middle Ages, the Byzantine Empire was prospering, especially for a few hundreds of years after its formation. Emperor St. Constantine (the Orthodox Church had sainted him) stopped all persecutions against Christians, made Christianity the state religion, and made Constantinople the central area of the Christian Church's growth and development. Thus, the first few ecumenical councils of the Christian Church were held in the Byzantine Empire with its emperor as the mover and shaker of religion. One of the more important things that happened was the building of churches; as a serious example, let's take a look at Hagia Sophia: St. Constantine built the first structure of that name, which had burned down in 415 A. D. It was replaced by Emperor St. Justinian (483-565) and consecrated in 537 A. D. When he saw it finished, he apparently exclaimed, "Oh, Solomon! I have surpassed thee!" Justinian was a pious and wise emperor; among the many things he had developed is what we now call the Roman legal system ("Corpus Juris Civilis"), and composed many prayers, among which "Only begotten Son and immortal word of God... " is sung at every Orthodox liturgy. Saint Sophia was the first Christian church which was converted to a mosque by the Turks after they captured Constantinople in 1452-1453 A. D; they also added 4 minarets and a few other structures to the church, and close by, the Turks built the Blue Mosque, which is flanked by 6 minarets, perhaps to outdo the structures at Hagia Sophia? I understand that there is "only" one mosque that has seven minarets, and it is in Saudi Arabia. Figures show the crowds of tourists visiting Hagia Sophia today. It has been a model for building many mosques in many countries. It and many other Byzantine churches are now museums, or at least one part of them are museums that contain icons and other components of the Byzantine Orthodox era. -

Many of us are unaware that Mary the mother of Jesus Christ lived much of her life after Her Son's crucifixion in a house near Ephesus owned by Apostle St. John. Jesus had instructed his disciple St. John to take care of His mother after His death. And St. John did. He had a house (or perhaps he had it built?) near Ephesus and She lived there until Her earthly death and apparent resurrection (the apostles buried Her, but when Her grave was opened a while later, she wasn't there). St. John's apparent grave near his house was opened in our era (19th century?), but it too was empty. It is known that he had traveled a lot (even went to the future land of Russia and predicted where Kiev was to be built), and it is likely that he died and was buried elsewhere.

Another interesting item to see in Istanbul is the drinking water cistern, which today is a show-tell item, but in ancient times, it was a drinking water reservoir for the city of Constantinople supplied by a system of water ducts. It was well built and decorated, with an impressive entry gate. It was improved and expanded by Roman emperor Justinian, because the population of Constantinople reached about 500,000 during his reign and all these people needed water, and technology at that time was not sufficiently advanced to drill deep wells to supply enough water as needed.

Greece is a major land in the East European/Western Asia region, whose recorded history lasts a long way from about 2000 B. C. to today. That's some 4000 years! And when the Byzantine Empire collapsed in 1453, the Turks did not stop there. They slowly were adding European countries to their conquests, including Greece, and succeeded in converting many Eastern European people into their Islamic religion. They conquered Greece, though the Greeks were quite resistant to becoming Moslem and in the early 19th century, they revolted and kicked out the Turks from their country. In addition, the Turks had been defeated in battle by Austrians and their allies, so that their expansion by the 19th century was stopped, and the conquered European folks were slowly regaining their freedoms, several of them by help from the Russians. Turkish expansion was totally stopped after World War I, when the Turks, allied with the Germans, were the War's losers. They became a republic, switched their capital city to Ankara from Istanbul, and were forced to keep only a small portion of European land surrounding the

Anatoly Bezkorovainy

city of Istanbul for themselves. And because of Greek initiatives as early as 1821 to free themselves from Turkish dominance (as well as their long history of influencing European culture in general), it became a leading nation in the Balkan area. Its capital city of Athens is one of the most important European cultural centers and a destination for millions of tourists who want to visit and admire the ancient Greek religious temples, sports arenas, and other public structures. My wife and I were among them at least twice, in 1999 and 2001.

In Athens we investigated that Acropolis hill that contains the temple of Parthenon and a number of other structures. Unfortunately, it was being restructured, so that admission into its inside was verboten. And the building on the side of Acropolis that has a side structure with the caryatides was also under repair. However, we did have a nice conversation with the local guide shown in all his national clothing glory. We visited the Tsarist Russian embassy grounds with the Russian Orthodox Church and a miniscule cemetery attached thereto which contained graves of the last Russian Imperial ambassador to Greece Count San Donato and his wife Sophia Demidova. We then walked to the cathedral square, where nuns were guarding doors of the cathedral and would not let in ladies (usually the tourist ones), who wore pants or shorts and had no kerchiefs on their heads. My wife met all their requirements and we were allowed in. We lit and installed candles before several icons and then went to the square, where buying and selling of stuff was going on in full speed. A salesman approached me and asked in Russian if I wanted to buy a fur coat. I said it was summer, so why would I want to do so. He answered that he will give it to me cheaply. And when I asked him how he knew that I understood Russian, he said that I looked like one. Amazing, but no sale! And so did a jewelry store salesman; we walked in there because I liked a wedding ring (Greek style) on exhibit in its window. And he too spoke Russian, and I bought the ring for Marilyn. Perhaps there are a lot of tourists in Greece from Russia.

Beyond the big cities that we visited in Greece and Turkey (Istanbul and Athens the Egyptian ones, we will mention below), we saw a plentiful group of smaller historic places and areas no less interesting than the big ones. Most of the time, we did not stay in their hotels, and did our sightseeing from the ship. The first one was Ephesus, in the Turkish country close to the port-city of Kusadasi. That's where our ship stopped and we were allowed to visit the ruins of a Roman city where St. Paul preached at one time and where the

Apostles were often visitors. It was a port city in Roman times, but the sea receded, the city basically died, and its port was replaced by a new town called Kusadasi on the new Mediterranean Sea coast. Ephesus became covered with sand and dust, only to be rediscovered by a British engineer who was building a railroad for the Turks in the area in 1860's. Little by little, the old city of Ephesus is being recovered, with many buildings or their parts still standing erect, for instance the "library". We visited the ancient city twice, in 1999 and 2001. An island called Santorini, is in Greek territory and is a huge tourist attraction. Our ship had to drop the anchor outside the coast and take us passengers to the island with motorboats. Once ashore, we had to climb to the town of Fira some 1500 feet higher than the coast, or else one could hire horses or mules and ride up the mountain in relative comfort. Today, there is a cable car that can take you up there, as far as I have been told. Santorini (also called Thera) is a beautiful place, with a great climate, and nice people. After we got home, our son Gregory went there with his classmate (male) to see how true our stories were, and fell in love with the place. He and his friend decided to buy a restaurant there and make the place their homes. They had $80,000 to spend, but the seller wanted $100,000 and wouldn't budge from that figure; thus, no deal, and they went home to the U.S. Greg got married and soon had two kids with his wife, and I don't know what happened to his friend. I wonder what would have happened if the seller had agreed to take the $80,000; would Greg move to live in Santorini? If he did, perhaps Marilyn and I would have joined him, and I would still be washing dishes in his restaurant.

But Santorini has an interesting history. Some 1000-2000 years B. C. (if I am not mistaken), the island was hit by a huge volcanic eruption which split the island into several parts and wiped out practically all life thereunto. That volcano is still smoking on a small island not too far from the main Santorini Island. Some years ago, a Santorini farmer was chasing a domestic animal of his1who had escaped from the ham or a fenced yard and saw it suddenly disappearing into the ground. He of course investigated, and found his bovine beast in a big hole with collapsed ground with some buildings in it. The beast had found the lost "city" of Akrotiri that disappeared under earth and ashes rained upon the ground after a volcanic eruption. Of course, the archeologists started digging and uncovered a town under the surface of the field. They are still digging there, but, unlike the case with Pompeii, no human remains were found there. The Akrotiri inhabitants must have left their island homes before the eruption and sailed away to elsewhere. Some wall paintings done by such former inhabitants have been found. Some folks have supposed that the Akrotiri residents may have sailed away as far as Palestine, and had settled on the shores of the Mediterranean Sea close to where the biblical Israelis were the inhabitants. And thus, they may have been the biblical Canaanites, the pagan scourge that the Israelis had to fight with.

The ship that we picked up to sail was supposed to go to Palestine, where the Akrotiri's inhabitants might have fled from the expected eruption of the nearby volcano. But the modem war of Israelis and Palestinians had heated up and the ship failed to anchor anywhere near modem Israel. Instead, its owners decided to visit some of that multitude of islands that exist in the Aegean Sea, some small and some large, and which certainly have had a number of magnificent cultures over the thousands of years of their existence, usually similar to those of the ancient Athenians, Spartans, Corinthians, and other Greek folks. And so we first stopped on the Island of Rhodes, which is located just a few miles from the Turkish shore, but is thoroughly Greek. It was the location of one of the ancient seven wonders of the world, Colossus of Rhodes, which was built in 280 B. C. and was "over 100 feet tall". It apparently served as a beacon for Rhodes harbor. It was destroyed by an earthquake around 226 B. C., and was never rebuilt. Phoenicians and Dorians came to Rhodes apparently before 1184 B. C. Its most ancient cities were Lindus, Camirus, and Halieia. Rhodes City was founded in the 4th century B. C. The Citadel of Rhodes was built by the Hospitaller knights in the Middle Ages of the current era, but the Moslem Turks took over the island in 1522 and owned it until 1912 when the Italians took over. They were followed by the Germans in 1943, then the British in 1945, and finally the Greeks in 1948.

The island of Crete was the place of perhaps the "oldest advanced civilization of Europe". Apparently it was the first culture to use the written language. This ("Minoan") culture existed, some say, between 3000 B. C. and 1100 B. C. The most famous personality there was King Minos, and one of their most important deities was apparently the bull. The buildings that survive the ages since the "Minoan" civilization are obvious that architectural arch had not yet been invented. Another Greek island with a history is Cyprus, part of which is owned by the Turkey but most of which is an independent nation with a population that is some 80% Greeks, The human race has been around there since 9700 years B. C., though writing on the island was not practiced until 1600 B. C. It was acquired by the Roman Empire in 58 B. C. St. Paul brought Christianity to them, and Cyprus became the first land whose leader was a Christian. It fell to the Turks in 1571, until World War I when Britain acquired the island. Today, it is divided into an independent Greek-speaking country (80%) and a Turkish-owned land. Cyprus has been a part of many civilizations: ancient Egypt, Persia, Greece, Roman Empire, and since 1960, independent. As I recall, we visited Cyprus on a Sunday, and were able to attend a liturgy in an Orthodox church, which was packed with worshippers. On the side of the square were some restaurants and other businesses with tables, at several of which were groups of elderly men playing chess or some other games. I assumed that they were doing that because the church was too crowded to get in; but we managed somehow.

For a while, let us step aside from the Greek islands and go back to its mainland, this time the Peloponnese peninsula There were a couple interesting places visited by our ship, such as Nafplion, which was Greek capitol city after they gained independence from the Turks (1823-1834), and nearby towns of Epidavros and Mykenai (Mycenae). A most interesting town nearby is Corinth, which controls the Corinth Canal, a very busy transit route for ships. It was a capital city of the Corinthian mini-state in 400 B. C., when its population number was 90,000. Today, it is 28,000. Apostle Paul visited Corinth 3 times, and wrote the Corinthians 3 letters, which are components of the New Testament. The church reminds one of Hagia Sophia. The city is situated on the 4-erie canal, which connects the Gulf of Corinth with the Saronic Gulf of the Aegean Sea.

The last country we visited during our 2001 voyage was Egypt. The ship docked at the Alexandria harbor, and we visited a number of points of interest in that city, including ancient harbor defense structures and some museums. On the next day, we got on the buses and drove to Cairo and the nearby area with ancient pyramids. Each bus had an armed guard accompanying us; the powers that be were afraid of insurgent attacks, which had occurred against tourists previously, perhaps to prevent the current Egyptian regime from making money from tourism. But nothing happened to us, and we had a grand time exploring the pyramids and other nearby structures. Along with exploring the pyramids and the sphinx, we got a chance to ride camels, that is, Marilyn did so with great joy; I was afraid of getting sea sick and just took a picture sitting on a stationary camel. The sphinx was much bigger than I had imagined previously, and was quite impressive, so that I acquired several pictures thereof. I am still wondering whether or not there is an interior in the sphinx, or is it all solid rock? It is big enough to be somewhat hollow, but nobody knew anything about that beyond that small room at the bottom front of the statue. After our visits with the pyramids and the sphinx, we drove to the Cairo Museum, and saw a multitude of mummies of pharaohs and other ancient Egyptian men of stature, including that of Ramses II and Tut Ankh Amen; the latter we had met before in Chicago's Natural History Museum some years ago. We also saw the famous Rosetta Stone, which was discovered some 200 years ago in Egypt, and since it was executed in two languages (ancient Egyptian hieroglyphs and Greek), it allowed the modern man to finally understand ancient Egyptian script, since Greek writing was well familiar to the Europeans. A figure shows a Cairo Egyptian cat, who was following us around the Cairo Museum and allowed Marilyn to pet it. Perhaps it was some re-incarnated ancient Egyptian personality who was hanging around in the form of a cat to meet the American tourists. The Egyptian experience was the last one for us on this trip, and as I recall, we went back to Athens to catch a plane for the USA. Our next journey was a year later, that time, to Western Europe.

And so, our next and last trip to Western Europe took place in the year 2002. We were accompanied by our good friend Beverley Dubin, who was with us when we were visiting Eastern Europe and Egypt. This time, Marilyn was healthy, her cancer was gone, and the doctors were certain that she was free of it. In fact, after the surgery she looked so good that the originally anticipated X-ray therapy was judged to be unnecessary. And the doctors were right; Marilyn's cancer never returned. Unfortunately, Marilyn managed to pick up another problem some years ago, but when one is nearing the age of 80, anything can happen, and at this time we were dealing with Parkinson's disease. But let's get back to 2002 A. D. We were settled in a small hotel in Rome's neighborhood of foreign embassies. The hotel was not plush, yet quite comfortable and well managed. It did not have a full restaurant, but we found one a few blocks away, where, unlike in Paris, the owners were very nice and helpful, they spoke English, and assisted us with choosing wines and Italian meals. And the restaurant's entertainer was willingly singing Italian songs for us. It was a pleasure to visit that place as long as we stayed in Rome. An interesting "event" occurred in our hotel, I believe on the second or third day of our stay there, when we observed an enormous amount of activity in the hotel hall lasting about one day and night. There were a bunch of men, all smoking cigarettes, running around, calling someone on cell phones, yelling, etc. And then, all suddenly, everything quieted down. We eventually found out that the president of Afghanistan was staying in our hotel for one night, I believe on the floor above us, and that all the activity we observed was created by the Italian secret service men who were supposed to protect him. They weren't very secret, however. Otherwise, the hotel stay was very pleasant.

In Rome, we visited a number of their historical structures, as well as places of current importance, especially the Vatican, "Citta del Vaticano." It is an independent nation within the boundaries of Rome, the capital of Italy. We went to St. Peter's cathedral, the principal building in the Vatican, but we weren't allowed to go into the lower levels where the resting areas of Christian saints are located. St. Peter's church is a huge place, bigger than Christ the Savior Cathedral in Moscow, perhaps the largest Christian church in the world. It was guarded by the Swiss guards, whose uniforms looked to me like clowns' dressings, but that's how they looked apparently in the Middle Ages. We marveled at the art in Vatican museums and chapels which are known all over the world, but still, one is awed when one sees the art in real life. Altogether, we were 3 days in Rome, and saw numerous structures that are famous as well as infamous. One such place was the Roman Colosseum where the masses were being entertained with gladiator fights or other deadly games. Next to the huge Colosseum stands the smallish Arch of St. Constantine built in memory of St. Constantine, who was the Caesar of Rome, and then changed his capital to Constantinople. After 3 days in Rome, we were taken to Civitavecchia, Rome's harbor city, to embark on the Crown Odyssey ship, where we would spend the rest of our voyage to Italy and its neighboring countries. The ship's owners are the Orient Lines that run a number of travel plans in Europe and other areas. Our next stop was Sorrento, Italy which included Capri and the ancient Roman city of Pompeii, which was destroyed by the eruption of the nearby Mt. Vesuvius volcano in 79 A. D.

Pompeii, unlike Santorini's Akrotiri, had apparently no warning that Vesuvius was going to erupt, and had thus caught many of its inhabitants unexpectedly. When Pompeii was rediscovered in the 1700's of this era, many human bodies were found as the debris was cleaned up. Some of them were copied by the gypsum technique. Pompeii must have been a city of the upper middle-class considering some of the beautiful brickwork and tiled floors found in their buildings. But the city's structures look like those after an American-British bombing of a German city in World War II. Beverley and Marilyn took a lunch break in Pompeii, and after a short stop in Naples, where I took a picture, our ship sailed to Sicily. That island, with Palermo as its capital, has a complicated history starting with its establishment by Phoenicians in the 8th century B. C., then a takeover by Greeks, Byzantium, and Moslem Arabs. Their first Christian faith was Byzantine Orthodoxy, and when the Muslims were kicked out, Roman Catholics took over. But many churches still carry their initial Byzantine properties, e. g., Monreale's cathedral, or Palermo's Nativity Church, and Palatine Chapel with icons of Sts. Gregory, Basil, and John Chrysostom. We took several photos of ourselves in Palermo, and then moved on to Malta. It used to be a British colony but now it is an independent entity. It lists the city of Mdina, location of "the original glass of Malta " manufacturing plant, but I could not find it on a map. Another photo I brought home was of a bunch of British soldiers gathered around an unexploded bomb. I imagine it was some bomb dropped on Malta's naval base by German aircraft during World War II. Some other Maltese buildings are shown in a building in the capital Valletta, which has an icon hanging on the wall, and has a sign saying no parking on the main square. The others are an entrance to the knights' church and a chapel on the seashore. Which knights they were in Malta it did not say, but most likely they were also in Palestine at one time, so like other such groups they were kicked out from there by the Muslims, and had settled in Malta.

The next stop on our sailing voyage was Corfu Island, which belongs to Greece, is populated by Greeks, and is possibly the westernmost part of Greece in Europe. So their culture is related to some extent to the Italian one, because for many years they were under the Venetian influence while the rest of Greece was under the Turkish power. Nevertheless, their religion remained Orthodox like it is in mainland Greece; on the island there is also an influential monastery and St. Spyridon is their beloved patron saint. The next stop of the ship was in Dubrovnik, Croatia, a true medieval city of Roman Catholic culture. And the last was Venice, where we were let out of the ship to visit the St. Mark's Cathedral, which, we were told, held a multitude of valuable items that the Western crusader knights had robbed from Constantinople when they were retreating from Palestine under

Moslem pressures. But the place was so crowded and the line trying to get into the church was so long that we were told by the church officials that it was unlikely that we would get in there that day. So we mingled among members of the crowd on St. Mark's square, visited their stores, and basically killed time until we were to go back to the ship. And the next day was our trip's last day, and our visit to Europe thus came to an end. Bon voyage home!

This trip to Italy was our last visit to Western Europe. I believe that we visited Russia and Eastern Europe again some 2-3 times after this one, as described in Chapter 3. The most memorable one was in 2004 in connection with the return 9f the Tikhvin Mother of God icon from Chicago to Russia, but after around 2007 we settled permanently in Galena and did not travel abroad because Marilyn came down with Parkinson's disease. We had to leave Galena eventually to stay in Arizona where our son Alex was living, where we had some moral and physical assistance from a close relative. I will write a few things about that in the last chapter of this book.

CHAPTER 5

TRAVELS TO COUNTRIES ON 3 CONTINENTS

Sometime in 1998, I received an invitation from Israel to go to an Israel city in 1999 and participate in an international biochemical conference (I don't remember what it was supposed to be called), but it was supposed to be on the topic of our department's research project. The talk was to last some 30-45 minutes and ended with questions by the listeners' biochemists. About a dozen biochemists were to be invited to the conference, which would last for 4-5 days (as I recall). The conference was to take place in the summer of 1999. I did of course agree to attend and to give a paper on my laboratory's results, and I also expected to take Marilyn with me, who would enjoy visiting Israel and the neighboring countries that I expected to attend. The entire trip was expected to last 3–4-weeks and we expected to attend several countries in Europe and the Middle East. However, our trip turned out to be somewhat different. Israel got information that its Arab enemies were not willing to see a foreign conference controlled by Israel and promised that they would kill all the conference members if it was held in Israel. The conference was dropped by Israel and made a promise to organize again when times are more peaceful. The ship's folks dropped the trip to Israel and changed the trip without stopping in Israel. Instead, they promised to visit other areas in the Middle East, without giving biochemical seminars anywhere. Marilyn and I decided to remain on the trip and to visit several other countries without Israel. The trip still turned out to be terrific.

CHAPTER 6

MARRIED LIFE OF MARILYN AND ANATOLY

The intent of this book is to summarize the events and experiences of the author's 88 years of life and put them in print to inform his descendants of what has happened during his and his ancestors' lives in Europe and the U.S. It is the author's great pity that his father, lgnaty Bezkorovainy, who was a well-educated persona, never bothered to write a story of his and his family's life, or even talk about it, since he lived through such a serious and important world's span of life like 19th and 20th centuries: World War I, Russian Revolution, independent Latvia's 22 years (1918-1940), Second World War, and life in post-World War II twenty-five years in America with his family. In fact, he didn't even like to tell stories of his interesting life events. To substitute a small way, to my father's inaction, I have written this book and a couple of previous ones (e.g., "All Was Not Lost," AuthorHouse publisher, 2008), which in a small way, may act as substitutes of my father's inaction (God bless his soul).

Our family, my father lgnaty, mother Olga, my brother, and I came to America in 19LmGermany To Germany, we came from my native city of Riga, Latvia in 1944 during World War II as Soviet armies were nearing the city of Riga, my birth place, in September, 1944. We could not stay in Soviet Latvia under the Soviet regime because my father was on the Bolshevik list to get arrested and sent to Siberia for the usual 10 years, if one could live that long while working in Soviet North Poles' labor camps. Why? Because during the Russian civil war in 1919, my father had been drafted into the White (anticommunist) army under Admiral Kolchak in Perm, Russia, where my father normally lived and studied medicine at the Perm University. In 1920, he managed to flee from Russia (which had become the Soviet Union) to independent Latvia, where he was married in 1930 to Olga Solovey-Pavlichenko, and my brother and I were born in 1938 and 1935 respectively.

And when the Bolsheviks had occupied Latvia in 1940, they remembered who my father was, but had not the time to arrest him and punish him for being a few months in Perm's White Army garrison (and perhaps the entire family as well) to send us to Siberia for 10 years, where we probably would not had survived. And so, we had to go to Germany to avoid Siberia with some 10 to 15% of Latvian population which did likewise late in the 1944th year. After the war, we and our fellow refugees were collected by the western Germany's occupiers (U.S., England, and France) into the so-called DP camps, and from there they emigrated to various "Western" countries such as Canada, Australia, Brazil, Argentina, and especially the U.S. The Bezkorovainys were fortunate to get to the U.S. in 1951. My mother's sister and her family came to the U.S. in 1949, relatively early because Mr. John Kijauskas had relatives in Chicago. And we ended up in Chicago as well because our first aim was Wilkes-Barre, Pennsylvania, where my father could not get a job and after a few months there, we moved to Chicago, where both of my parents died in their older years. I received my education in Chicago worked there as a biochemist for some 43 years, married my wife Marilyn (she had 2 sons with me), we retired in 2005 to Galena, Illinois, and in 2015 moved to Sun Lakes, Arizona, where in 2020 Marilyn passed away and I remained alive to write stories as late as today: 2023 A. D. at the age of 88.

And so in America, I, Anatoly Bezkorovainy, graduated from high school in 1953 (I was 18), then from University of Chicago with a BS in Biochemistry in 1956. In September of 1956, I started the study for the Ph.D. degree at the University of Illinois Medical College, which I finished in September of 1960 and went to Oak Ridge, Tennessee laboratory for postdoctoral work. The Ph. D. degree was officially granted to me in June, 1961. On Easter day, in the spring of 1960, we celebrated the feast and after the church service, in the home of our friends, where we met the Grib family that consisted of Nicholas and Paula Grib and their daughter Marilyn. I liked Marilyn a lot, and later I had asked George if he was interested in her. He said no; he already had a girlfriend whom he liked a lot. So I called Marilyn and took her on a date. At that time, I was involved to some extent with a girl named Gertrude, but Marilyn seemed to be more interesting, and in addition, she was of my religion. So we dated occasionally, but I was busy at that time finishing my studies and research at the University of Illinois, so I did not date too frequently. In fall of 1960, I had my thesis exam, I passed it, and was admitted to a post-doctoral job at the Oak Ridge atomic bombs laboratory. Officially, I got my Ph.D. degree in June, 1961 because the University of Illinois was granting degrees only once a year: in the June of each year. I came to Chicago on the day I received my Ph. D. diploma, and as I remember, I took Marilyn on a date on that day to celebrate my success. It was a successful meeting, and I dated her every time I came to Chicago to visit my parents, either from Oak Ridge or from Ames, Iowa, where I went to work in September of 1961 at the U.S. Animal Disease Laboratory. After a year at Oak Ridge and. a year in Ames, Iowa (1960-1962), I returned to Chicago to work at the Rush-Presbyterian-St. Luke's Hospital, which organized the Rush Medical College, where I became a professor, staying there until my retirement in 2005. I was 43 years at the Rush Medical School/ Hospital! And thus in the year of 1962, I returned to Chicago and started seriously dating Marilyn, so that in the year of 1963 I asked Marilyn to marry me. I was 28 years old, and Marilyn was 25; it was thus time for the both of us to get married.

Thus, in 1963, I asked Marilyn to marry me. She said yes, but a year later. I was surprised that she wanted such a long wait, but I said OK and I bought her an engagement ring that she liked and wore it until she was buried in the year of 2020; that's 57 years. So, in June 1964, Marilyn and I were married at Holy Trinity Cathedral at Chicago by Archbishop John, who at that time was a Bishop of the Midwest in the Orthodox Church of America. This church was established in Alaska by the Russians when they "discovered" and occupied Alaska at the end of the 18th century. Incidentally, I am still surprised why the Brits, who owned Canada after the American revolution in 1776, did not attach Alaska to Canada or establish a separate colony, but they didn't, and the Russians did, since it was just across the sea passage from Siberia. The Russians discovered and occupied Alaska at the end of the 18th century; it was just across the Alaskan pathway between Asia where Russia was and America, where Alaska was no one's colony north of Canada. Why that land was not owned by the Brits who owned Canada just south of Alaska I still can't understand. So the Russians claimed Alaska at the end of 18th century and established Sitka as their capital; they also established the Russian Orthodox Church to change and serve the Alaskan natives from their pagan religions to the Orthodox one. The main Orthodox church was set up and is still functioning in Sitka, Alaska, and it was responsible for expanding the Orthodox Church along the Pacific Ocean south into the Spanish California, which eventually became part of the U.S. Thus, today's Orthodox Church of America, to which we belong, was brought from Russia to Alaska and then to the United States; since the 18th century, there were a number of Alaskan Orthodox priests joined to the Russian Orthodox Church's sainthood. It thus has an important religious history to which we now belong. Our son Alexander was baptized at the Holy Trinity Cathedral, whereas Gregory was baptized in Holy Virgin Protection Church, both in Chicago.

In 2018, in a book entitled "A lifetime of Achievement: Our Collection of Prestigious listees," on page 181, appeared an article entitled "Medicine and Health Care," Anatoly Bezkorovainy. The article were as follows:

"A widely regarded educator, Anatoly Bezkorovainy, JD, Ph.D., served as a faculty member with the Rush University Medical Center for more than half a century prior to his retirement in 2005. During this time, he was recognized as an associate chairman and director of educational programs with the Biochemistry Department, among other prestigious roles. Although his involvement with the R University Medical Center spanned nearly the entirety of his professional career, Dr. Bezkorovainy is known for holding a variety of additional positions related to his area of expertise.

"Early in his career, Dr. Bezkorovainy attended the University of Chicago, where he received a Bachelor of Science in 1956. Upon completing a Ph. D. through the University of Illinois in 1960, he joined the Oak Ridge National laboratory as a research associate. Dr. Bezkorovainy held this position for one year before assuming the role of chemist with the United States Department of Agriculture. Since joining the Rush University Medical Center as an assistant professor in 1962, Dr. Bezkorovainy has filled numerous academic roles related to his fields of focus. Within five years of joining the university, he was recognized as an associate professor, a position he held until he was promoted to the rank of professor of biochemistry in 1973. At this time, Dr. Bezkorovainy chose to continue expanding the scope of his knowledge by pursuing postgraduate education.

"Upon receiving a JD through the Illinois Institute of Technology in 1977, Dr. Bezkorovainy was admitted to practice in Illinois. Beginning 1980, he was recognized as an associate chairman and director of educational programs with the Biochemistry Department of the Rush University Medical Center for two decades. A dedicated researcher, Dr. Bezkorovainy has received numerous grants from National Science Foundation, National Institutes of Health, American Heart Association, and Industrial Institutions.

"Although Dr. Bezkorovainy Officially retired in 2005, he continues to maintain involvement with a variety of industry organizations, including the American Chemical Society, American Society of Biological Chemists, American Dairy Science Association, National Science Foundation, National Institutes of Health and American Heart Association. He previously served as a lecturer with the Dr. William M. Scholl College of Podiatric Medicine in North Chicago, between 2000 and 2008.

"In addition his status as a lifetime Achiever, Dr. Bezkorovainy has been featured in a wide range of honor publications: Who's Who in America, including the 71st edition of the series; Who's Who in Education; Who's Who in Medicine and Healthcare; Who's Who in Science and Engineering; Who's who in the Midwest; and Who's Who in the World. In recognition of his commitment to the continued pursuit of scientific research and development, Dr. Bezkorovainy was awarded a 50-Year Member Award from the American Chemical Society.

"A respected voice in the academic community, Dr. Bezkorovainy has authored a variety of written works that serve as a testament to his knowledge and experience as a scholar and educator. His most recent publications include "History of Imperial Russia," which was published in 2014, and "All Was Not Lost," which was published in 2008. In addition, Dr. Bezkorovainy is credited as a co-author of "Concise Biochemistry," "Biochemistry and Physiology of Bifidobacteria," "Basic Biochemistry," and "Basic Protein

Chemistry." A known contributor of articles to professional journals, Dr. Bezkorovainy also authored "Biochemistry of Non-Heme Iron," which was published in 1980. In 2015, he was recognized as a translator for "I Have Received Much More Than I Have Deserved." His latest book, "Science and Medicine in Imperial Russia," is scheduled to be published in 2018 by Lulu Press.

This above two-page narrative was printed in a 2018 issue of the "Marquis Who's Who" book by Albert Nelson Marquis. It basically indicated, very briefly albeit, what were my activities in my 50+ working years in the area of my professional work, and why my persona was mentioned in the Marquis Who's Who. I have described much of my lifetime above, and in this chapter, I will briefly relate the summaries of the rather numerous books that I had published in my 50+ year working life. And here goes: the very first book I published was "Basic Protein Chemistry," with me the only author. I wrote it because I gave the graduate students a course on protein chemistry and biochemistry after they had taken the basic biochemistry courses and I could not find a proper advanced text book on protein chemistry in the English Language. Its title was "Basic Protein Chemistry," and it had 232 pages. With hard covers, as I remember, it cost $20. One critique by a book reviewer was that I had an error in an ultracentrifugation equation, which I could not find, but otherwise the book was OK. Neither for this book, nor for future others did I get any money; I believe that the publisher (Charles C. Thomas, Springfield, Illinois) gave me a couple hundred dollars and that was it. It just about paid for what I paid to write the book. This first book of mine was published in 1970. I did not do its second edition, but it is lots of fun (at least for me) to look through it every once in a while: the first book that I ever published.

The above-mentioned "Basic Protein Chemistry" book was the first book that I had ever written. I had already written many research papers at that time. This was in the 1970's year A.D., thirty five years after my birth. Before that, I hadn't written any books whatever, and thus it was an important "numero uno" among the other books that followed in my life, including the 1992 book "A History of Holy Trinity Russian Orthodox Cathedral of Chicago 1892-1992," which was published for a celebration of the 100th year of the Cathedral's existence. I was 57-years old and only 8 years from my semi-retirement at 65 in the year of 2000, and prior to that I had already published several other books on Biochemistry topics. But I consider this one:(ISBN 0-9632743-0-9) as the most important of my books that I ever published because it has something to do with eternity rather than a human life span. The book has about 150 pages and an 8 1/2 x 11 inch size. There are a multitude of photographs in full color in the book. I had ordered 1000 books to be published; the church sold them $30 each and I doubt that there are any left for sale. Several authors were involved, who all knew what they were writing about (I hope!): "One Hundred Years of Service to God and Man" by Anatoly Bezkorovainy (pp.1- 62); "A Cloud of Witnesses" by Thomas Klocek (pp. 63-86); "Sacred Song at Holy Trinity Cathedral" by Leonard Soroka (pp. 87-98); "Iconography of Holy Trinity Cathedral" by Matushka Alexandra Garklavs (pp. 99-130); "The Architecture of Holy Trinity Cathedral" by Charles E. Gregersen (pp.131-140); and "The Present and Future State of Orthodoxy in America" by Roderick F. Mollison (pp. 141-144). His Beatitude Metropolitan Theodosius wrote the Foreword (page ix), and Preface (pages xi to xiv) were written by Anatoly Bezkorovainy.

To continue discussing the books I had written either by myself with co-authors, my next one herewith is a text-book published in 1980 by my two professorial colleagues and myself. Drs. Max Rafelson and Jim Hayashi, both my fellow members of the Biochemistry Department of Rush Presbyterian-St. Luke's Medical Center, had already written and published three previous editions of this relatively small and concise text-book with a third co-author by the name of Dr. Steven Binkley of the University of Illinois Medical School. I was his replacement for the fourth edition in 1980 after he had retired from work. It was printed by MacMillan Publishing Co. Dr. Hayashi retired shortly thereafter, and perhaps the publisher did not get enough benefit from the book's sales because he did not ask us to write the fifth edition after 5-6 years of its use. But we were offered to provide the fifth edition by the Marcel Decker Co. Dr. Rafelson wasn't terribly happy to again work on it; he had been promoted to a deanship and was fairly close to retirement; so I took over the job of getting the book organized with Dr. Rafelson to write perhaps a few chapters for the book. It was printed in 1996, and the text consisted of 600 pages (compared to 400 in the previous text). It was no longer a quick review booklet; I thought; that we covered everything that the medical students should know at that level reasonably well. Still it was quite short compared to those of other authors' that I had seen. We named our book "Concise Biochemistry." The text is available with a 40-page booklet named "Solutions Manual." It has answers and explanations for problems that the book has at the end of each chapter. I don't know if the store charges extra money for that booklet. Dr. Rafelson and I were very proud of the book and at least I believed at the time I had it printed that it was the best teaching item that I had ever published. I don't know if our Rush medical students and biochemistry fellow professors agreed; I stopped being the biochemistry course director when I semi-retired in June of 2000.

Since my student days, I was interested in the biochemistry of iron and proteins such as hemoglobin, transferrin, ferritin, conalbumin, etc., and decided to write (someday) a book on iron biochemistry, even if it might take years to accomplish such a task. In fact, I was conducting research on transferrin (a plasma protein that binds iron via its amino acid side chains rather than via heme like hemoglobin) when the opportunity appeared: my acquaintance, Dr. Earl Frieden of Florida State University, needed to organize writing books on proteins that bind external materials; and for iron, there was one book that was to be written on proteins that bind iron via heme and another group that binds iron without heme. And he chose me for the latter type of book, because he had read my papers on transferrin, a plasma protein that binds iron via amino acid side-chains. The book has 9 chapters, of which I wrote eight, and my colleague, Dr. Dorice Narins, wrote one chapter "Absorption of Non-Heme Iron." The book has a total of 435 pages, and was published in 1980 by Plenum Press.

The last biochemical book that I published in 1989 was "Biochemistry and Physiology of Bifidobacteria" by CRC Press of Boca Raton, Fla. Two of its chapters were written by Dr. Robin Miller Catchpole, M. D., who was my Ph. D. student. The book has 226 pages and a total of 8 chapters. Its size is large, 7 x 10 inches. My co-author received her Ph. D. post mortem, God bless her soul!

This ends the list of my scientific publications. A somewhat larger number of books is non-science in nature and are listed below.

In my life as a professor of biochemistry I had managed to write a number of books with or without co-authors, though all of the are published with my name as one of the authors There were, as I recall, several types of books that I had written that meant for two purposes: the role of biochemistry to determine the biochemical issues that control the lives of human beings, and then such issues that already have been determined and are now being taught to future physicians. Some books that I had written were authored by myself alone, but several others have co-authors with my name to whom I am exceedingly grateful, because their ideas and knowledge are unique and without them it would not be possible for me to write all these biochemical texts.

There were only five books that directly concerned the topic of my profession of biochemistry, and all of them but one was done with co-authors; or I could better say, for whom I was a co-author. The book with my name only was "Basic Protein Chemistry" (my first book that I ever published) (in 1970). Its purpose was to give medical and graduate students a course in advanced protein chemistry after they had the basic 2 quarters of biochemistry required by the medical school, i.e., its t o basic biochemistry courses. Medical students did not have to take this course, but our graduate students did. This was the first book I had ever written and I was very proud of it; Basic Protein Chemistry, 230 pages; my first book I had ever written.

I have written it and published it because my chairman gave me the orders to provide a graduate level protein chemistry course for our department graduate students. He had probably observed graduate students to take the two medical curriculum courses with the medical students, but after that, they knew very little on protein chemistry and to work with them, as well as many other non-medical issues was difficult and I could not find an existent text-book on protein chemistry with which to teach protein chemistry even to our graduate students. Therefore, I wrote my own book and had it published in 1970 by Charles C. Thomas Company. As I remember, it cost $23 for each student. I got no money for writing this book, nor any other book that I ever published, either for students or university courses that I taught. This first book, "Basic Protein Chemistry," was followed by other biochemistry texts plus or minus a couple. For all these books I did not earn a penny; I, however, was happy enough to see my works published by American publishers. Yet before retirement I managed to become an author on only 4 books. All four were on biochemistry topics, and all but one had several authors with me as the principal one. Two were text-books for medical students who were taking two quarters of biochemistry in their first year of medical school. Another biochemistry was a text that I partially wrote with Dr. Rafelson. Its title was Concise Biochemistry published in 1996; it had 610 pages and was meant as a text for future doctors. Associated with this book we also published "Concise Biochemistry Solutions Manual", which contained questions, problems, and summaries for each chapter (total of 40 pages). This, of course, was not a review book as "Basic Biochemistry" was. It was teaching and not a reviewing book in 1996, and I don't know if my professional followers used it after I retired in 2000.

The third biochemical book that I published with my co-author, Dr. Dorice Narins, who wrote the third chapter titled "Absorption of Non-Heme Iron" in a book titled "Biochemistry of Non-Heme Iron" with 430 pages; it was asked me to be written by Prof. Earl Frieden, who taught at the University of Florida; he planned to publish a number of biochemical texts that he ordered to do to his friends like me to write about all earthly elements, with at least one book for each element. So I agreed to write a book on biochemistry of non-heme iron, whereas he would write a book on heme-containing compounds. I don't know how many other biochemists agreed to write books on other elements, but in "Biochemistry of Nonheme Iron" with 440 pages Dorice Narins wrote a chapter (pp. 47-128) titled "Absorption of Nonheme Iron." And A. Bezkorovainy wrote the rest of the chapters' content.

The title of my 7-chapter book was 1. Tissue Iron and an Overview of Non-Heme Biochemistry; 2. Ferrokinetics; 3. Absorption of Non-heme Iron; 4. Chemistry and Metabolism of the Transferrins; 5. Chemistry and Biology of Iron Storage; 6. Interaction of Non-heme Iron with Immature Red Cells. 7. Microbial Iron Uptake and the Antimicrobial Properties of the Transferrins; 8. The Iron Sulfur Proteins and 9. Miscellaneous Aspects of Iron metabolism.

Chapter 3 was termed "Absorption of Non-heme Iron" and I left this to be done by Dr. Narins. I am still at my current 88th age status, and getting afraid with my age causing loss of writing abilities.

The last biochemistry book that I had written (Biochemistry and Physiology of Bifidobacteria") was with my graduate student Robin Miller-Catchpole, M.D., who wanted to get a Ph. D. degree in addition to her M.D. She wanted to be a professor in a medical school. She received the Ph. D. degree in biochemistry in 1989, a few months after she passed away. She had finished all Ph. D. requirements, but did not finish her dissertation. I applied our leadership to award her Ph. D. anyway, and they did, the Lord bless them. So the two of us wrote a book mentioned at the top of this paragraph, whose authors are listed A. Bezkorovainy and Robin Miller-Catchpole. The publisher was CRC Press, 1989. Robin of course did not have the time to write a dissertation, but during her work in my laboratory, she and I published a number of papers in biochemistry journals, which had enough work listed there to be able to write a dissertation. I believe that the book we published ("Biochemistry and Physiology of Bifidobacteria") could be used as a formal Ph. D. booklet. Robin's work was sufficiently described in there.

So the book published with Robin Miller-Catchpole was my last biochemistry book that I published in my working era (1960-2000 A. D.). Between the year of 2000 and 2Q23 (i.e. between my retirement in 2000 A. D. and today) I must have published some dozen + books, but they are not related much at all with biochemistry. Some stories are related to biochemistry, but very few are. But writing I did not quit after my retirement, and I have continued perhaps even in larger amounts.

At this point in June of 2000 A.D. I "retired" from my normal work at the medical school, and for the next 5 years, I gave lectures once a day at the Rush Medical College in the morning and gave a lecture every day in the afternoon at the Chicago Medical School. Both groups were first year medical students taking their normal biochemistry courses. I did this for 5 years (2000 to 2005). I did this for 5 years, still living in Chicago and having a cottage in Galena, Illinois, where we used to go on weekends and spend their time in summer when the medical schools were using their vacations. In 2005 summer, I quit all working projects; we bought a larger house in Galena Illinois with a 2-car garage and moved there "lock, stock, and barrel" from Chicago are Marilyn and I lived there for 10 years; for me, that was my most pleasant period of my life; most of the 10 years, at least! In fact, we were hoping to live there for the rest of our lives. But that did not happen; in 2010, Marilyn was diagnosed with Parkinson's Disease, which required us to move to some place where the doctors knew how to handle such a problem. Though they were able to diagnose Parkinson's Disease in a Dubuque hospital, they did not know how to treat it because Parkinson's Disease was almost unknown in Dubuque, Iowa and Galena Illinois areas; there were few if any genetics of that sort bn the Mississippi River shores of that area., Marilyn had such genetics because her parents were born in the White Russia area, where such genetics are prevalent. For 5 years after Marilyn was diagnosed with the disease, we stayed in Galena in our new house with a two-car garage because Marilyn's illness was processed very slowly and we didn't need super expert physicians to take care of her disease. But after 2010, Marilyn had to be treated by experts of Parkinson's Disease, and we decided to move, at least for a part of the year, where the Parkinson's Disease experts were not rare. We decided to move, for a part of the year, to the Phoenix, Arizona area where our son Alex lived and there was a Parkinson's Disease section in the Phoenix largest hospital. They knew how to treat Parkinson's Disease as well as anything in the world.

And so, in 2015, we bought a house in Sun Lakes, Arizona and for the next 2-3 years we moved there for winter times (we still did not wish to give up our house in Galena). But Marilyn's disease was moving faster and by 2017 or so, she became bedridden, we had to sell our Galena house, and move to Sun Lakes "lock, stock, and barrel." The local physicians tried to help her, but Marilyn's time (10 years) was really up, and she died in the fall of 2020 in the Phoenix "ancient" cemetery's section where Orthodox folks are generally buried. Bishop Daniel and Archpriest David Balmer were serving the panikhidas.

After my wife Marilyn died, I decided to write a book on her life. It turned out to be 2 books, relatively short both with about 150 pages each, yet somewhat different. They contain a huge number of pictures indicating various places where Marilyn and I had lived and where we had travelled. The other book was published in 2022 and contained more serious story tellings rather than pictures. The first Marilyn book has a title of "Marilyn the Mother, Wife, and Teacher," whereas the second has a more serious name "The Last Call." The readers may note that these two little books are no longer teachings of biochemistry. And in my retirement, I wrote a few more non-biochemistry books which were concerned with my travels and history of Russia. They were written by me after I retired from work at the medical school. I believe the first one was printed in 2008, "All Was Not Lost," with 674 pages, and printed by "authorHouse" publisher. It took me 3 years to write. It basically discussed my entire life-time starting with my grandfather on my father's side. He was a graduate of the Corps of Pages (the Russian officers' training school) and graduated from there in 1874. Instead of joining the army he joined, the trans-Siberian railroad building organization (I am not sure exactly what he was doing there), and retired when the railroad from Moscow to Vladivostok was finished in the beginning of the 20th century and joined his family in St. Petersburg, where he passed away in his 50's in the year of 1905. My father was only 5 years old at that time, but I believe that he was the youngest member of the family. My father's family moved there from St. Petersburg to Perm, where my grandma's dad was working as a priest at an Orthodox church, and she opened a shop where she was making and selling clothing for the city inhabitants. And that's where my father grew up, started medical school, but because of the Revolution, etc. had to leave Russia for Latvia, where in 1930 he married my mom Olga, and I was born in 1935. The book "All Was Not Lost" has all the details. So this story that I just described with a few sentences, plus the continuation for the rest of my life is described in a book that I published in 2008 by the name of "All was not Lost." At the end of the entire book I decided to mention all the rest of my books that I wrote after my retirement. I doubt if I will write anything beyond the book that I am finishing now. Another book that described some of my history via photographs was "Beyond All Was Not Lost," which also has some 500 pages, describing my and my wife's travels around the world. Most photos there are in color (I myself took most of them) and there are many of them in the book so that today, it costs $120 each. The pictures are largely from our trips in the 1970's to 1990's, mostly to give scientific papers at continents of the world, though most of our travels were only here in America and in Europe.

Another book of which I am quite proud was written and published by me in 2014; its title is "History of Imperial Russia," which has only 394 pages, but it seemed to me and others that it handled all of Russia's history until 1918 reasonably well. It was published by Lulu Enterprises, and an "expert" review that I saw was very good, I thought.

As a last thing I wish to mention a couple of books I published with the Lulu Enterprises group that likes to publish book interpretations from foreign languages. I published a few such books, but when I looked for them, I found only two. One was a translation from Russian to English by me. The author, Dr. Alexander Gavrilin who wrote the biography of Archbishop John Garklavs, who was a bishop in Latvia until 1944 when he, along with us and about 15% of the Latvian population, left during World War II to Germany as the Soviet troops were nearing, pushing the German army back to Germany. Bishop John Garklavs of Riga, along with the rest Latvian refugees, escaped to Germany with 25 Orthodox priests and the Tikhvin Mother of God Icon, which he took with him to Germany, then to the United States, where the famous icon stayed after the archbishop's death, and was returned to Russia in 2004 after Bishop John's death and conversion of Russia to non-communism. The Tikhvin icon was returned to Russia and was placed back to the rebuilt Tikhvin Monastery, where Ivan the Terrible of Russia ordered it to be placed and kept when it was found by Russian peasants in a forest of Northern Russia. The ruling tsar, Ivan the Terrible, ordered to build a monastery where the icon was found, and the icon was then kept and honored there by "all" Russians until the Bolshekivs put it in a museum, and during the WWII, the Germans took it to Riga and left it with Archbishop John then did it himself, then took it to the U.S., and it was ministered in the U.S. until 2004, when it was returned to Russia. My wife Marilyn and I accompanied it to Russia, where it is now staying in the rebuilt Tikhvin Monastery where it was since the times of Ivan the Terrible to the 1940s. The story of the icon is described in Dr. Gavrilin's book and its Russian translation by A. Bezkorovainy.

The other books of mine that I wish to mention were a collection of my publications that I had made over a long period of time during my activity as a researcher in the laboratory and the accomplishments of Russian chemists and biologists. I include physicians into the group of biologists. Thus, the book "Science and Medicine in Imperial Russia" has published a rather wide group of Russian biologists-doctors and scientist who had accomplished efforts in both biological sciences and medicine. The book "Science and Medicine in Imperial

Russia" was published in 2018 and was pretty much like a second edition of a book that I wrote in the 1980's. However, I have lost it and could not be making any comparisons between the two of them. And also, nobody accepted it for publication at that earlier time. The publishers maintained that chemistry and other sciences were unknown in Tsar's Russia; that there was nothing that could be described as Russian discovery during the tsarist era. The Soviets were the starters of all discoveries in Russia, according to them. But how come that there were no Nobel prize by Russians in medicine before the revolution in Russia? Such thinking was absolutely ridiculous by many earlier American scientists, and my 2018 books, as well as plenty of others have shown that scientist discoveries in Russia in the 19th century and the early 20th on were plentiful and of super importances for the world's human populace.

At this point I will finish writing about my scientific historical activities in Russia before the revolution. Perhaps my readers should attempt to study a book written by S. E. Shnoll (I read his Russian-language book printed in 1997) I don't know if there is an English translation thereof. It describes in Russian how the Soviets treated the sciences and the scientists. It was pathetic! They created their own sciences the Bolsheviks did! Many real scientists were killed, and many were able to escape to the Western world. One such American Russian invented a special type of gasoline that allowed American and British planes during World War II to fly pretty far into Germany and bomb their military establishments, thus winning World War II. There were several scientists in America and Western world who got away from the Soviets. The story of Russian Tsarist scientists, who escaped from Russia after the revolution has been told by many writer-authors, but it seems that they all have been Russians and wrote in the Russian language without much informing the western world. The Western world acquired many superb Russian scientists after the Communist revolution occurred in Russia; in that way, the revolution in Russia benefited the Western world in an important way. Yet no one recalls it or mentions it.

With this story, I will finish my book, which will, most likely, be the last story of my life's writings. I am close to being 89 years old after ending the story here, and I don't believe that I will be writing beyond this 2024th year. I think that my writing talent, whatever it had been, has disappeared and is not likely to recover. That's just fine; the one that I've had wasn't very successful; it cost me plenty of dollars, but I haven't earned a penny thereby.

Yet writing of it was plenty of fun and perhaps it had earned me a long life and to have a loving wife and two sons, Gregory and Alexander.

My loving wife Marilyn passed away in the year of 2020 after being ill for 10 years (2010 to 2020) of Parkinson's Disease. It is a genetic disease somewhat common in Belarus and Russia. Both of her parents had come to America from Belarus before the First World War, and my wife was born in Chicago in 1938. She passed away from a genetic disease which is impossible to cure. I wrote my wife's Marilyn biographical stories (2 booklets) after her demise, one published in 2021 and the other in 2022. The titles are "Marilyn the Mother, Wife Teacher" (2021) and "The Last Call" (2022). Both have about 150 pages with beautiful Marilyn's photographs on the covers. Author's Tranquility Press did a superb job. God bless Marilyn's soul! I am now waiting for one (or both) of my sons to write books about their lives and families like their father did. God bless the readers.

Fig. 6-1. Visiting St. Petersburg castle
of the tsar circa 2000 A.D.

Fig. 6-2. Around 2011 A.D. in a restaurant waiting to be seated in Pheonix. Marilyn and Anatoly standin, their bearded son with his wife and two daughters seated, and Alexander Bezkorovainy and the church deacon standing.

Fig. 6-3. Waiting to climb into a ship in the Mississippi
River in Dubuque, Iowa are Anatoly and Marilyn Bezkorovainy
and Father Sergei Garklavs with his wife around 2010.

Fig. 4. Anatoly with his grandchildren at a visitation
in Galena on 22 /1 /2014.

6-5. The 1986 Christmas fest by teachers of Marilyn's school including the nuns.

6-6. Marilyn riding a camel in Egypt's Sahara desert.

6-7. Anatoly and Marilyn near a major pyramid in Egypt

6.8. This year of 2000 was my "retirement" year. I was 65
years if age after Feb. 11. So they allowed me to lead my
students to get them their MD degrees. I was impressed!

6.9. Anatoly Bezkorovainy and Marilyn Grib were married on June 8, 1964. They celebrated 50 years together in 2014.

Fig. 6-10. The Bezkorovainys moved there around 2015 and Marilyn passed away in 2020. She is buried in the Orthodox section of its main cemetery.

Fig. 6-11. Grave of Marilyn Bezkorovainy